The People's Bible Teachings

HOLY SPIRIT

The Giver of Life

John F. Vogt

NORTHWESTERN PUBLISHING HOUSE
Milwaukee, Wisconsin

All Scripture quotations, unless otherwise indicated, are taken from the HOLY BIBLE, NEW INTERNATIONAL VERSION®. NIV®. Copyright © 1973, 1978, 1984 by International Bible Society. Used by permission of Zondervan Publishing House. All rights reserved.

The "NIV" and "New International Version" trademarks are registered in the United States Patent and Trademark Office by International Bible Society. Use of either trademark requires the permission of International Bible Society.

All rights reserved. No part of this publication may be reproduced, stored in a retrieval system, or transmitted in any form or by any means—electronic, mechanical, photocopy, recording, or otherwise—except for brief quotations in reviews, without prior permission from the publisher.

Library of Congress Card 97-66995
Northwestern Publishing House
1250 N. 113th St., Milwaukee, WI 53226-3284
© 1997 by Northwestern Publishing House.
Published 1997
Printed in the United States of America
ISBN 0-8100-0751-7

Table of Contents

Editor's Preface

The People's Bible Teachings is a series of books on all of the main doctrinal teachings of the Bible.

Following the pattern set by The People's Bible series, these books are written especially for laypeople. Theological terms, when used, are explained in everyday language so that people can understand them. The authors show how Christian doctrine is drawn directly from clear passages of Scripture and then how those doctrines apply to people's faith and life. Most importantly, these books show how every teaching of Scripture points to Christ, our only Savior.

The authors of The People's Bible Teachings are parish pastors and professors who have had years of experience teaching the Bible. They are men of scholarship and practical insight.

We take this opportunity to express our gratitude to Professor Leroy Dobberstein of Wisconsin Lutheran Seminary, Mequon, Wisconsin, and Professor Thomas Nass of Martin Luther College, New Ulm, Minnesota, for serving as consultants for this series. Their insights and assistance have been invaluable.

We pray that the Lord will use these volumes to help his people grow in their faith, knowledge, and understanding of his saving teachings, which he has revealed to us in the Bible. To God alone be the glory.

Curtis A. Jahn
Series Editor

Introduction

"I believe that I cannot by my own thinking or choosing believe in Jesus Christ, my Lord, or come to him," Martin Luther confessed in his explanation to the Third Article of the Apostles' Creed. I am saved only because "the Holy Spirit has called me by the gospel, enlightened me with his gifts, sanctified and kept me in the true faith."

Because the Holy Spirit plays such a vital role in God's plan of salvation, the Nicene Creed calls the Holy Spirit "the giver of life." The Spirit is active, powerful, and very much at work in God's people, giving them the life Jesus won for them. He brings us to faith and keeps us in faith, thereby giving us spiritual life, life lived in intimate fellowship with God as our Father.

As the Holy Spirit does his work, he doesn't call much attention to himself. Rather, he calls attention to Jesus, our Savior. In spite of this fact, the Holy Spirit has attracted quite a bit of attention throughout the history of the Christian church. He and his work even have been at the center of considerable controversy. Much of the controversy in the modern-day church revolves around the charismatic movement.

Christians view the Holy Spirit and his gifts differently. In this book we will look at what the Bible says about the points in controversy and find its answers to them. More importantly, I pray this book will help us grow in our knowledge of and closeness to the Holy Spirit. I pray the Holy Spirit will be not just a doctrine of our theology, but also the source of spiritual power for our lives.

1

His Divine Person

"Now this is the true Christian faith: We worship one God in three persons and three persons in one God, without mixing the persons or dividing the divine being. . . . So the Father is God, the Son is God, the Holy Spirit is God; yet they are not three Gods, but one God."[1] With these words the Athanasian Creed summarizes the Bible's teaching about the triune God.

There have always been some who reject this biblical doctrine. The Koran states: "So believe in Allah and His messengers, and say not 'Three'—Cease! (it is better for you!)—Allah is only One God."[2] The Church of Jesus Christ of Latter-day Saints (Mormon) teaches that Father, Son, and Holy Spirit are three separate and unequal gods and that by "eternal progression" humans can become gods too. Joseph Smith, that group's founder, wrote, "Jesus is greater than the Holy Spirit which is subject to him, but his Father is greater than he is!"[3] Joseph Rutherford, an early leader of the Jehovah's Witnesses, claimed, "The doctrine of the 'trinity' finds no support whatsoever in the Bible, but, on the contrary, the Bible proves beyond all doubt that it is the Devil's doctrine, fraudulently imposed upon man to destroy faith in Jehovah."[4] Denial of the Trinity by those outside the Christian church doesn't surprise us.

It may come as a surprise, however, to discover that Christians also are often unclear about the Holy Spirit's place in the Godhead. I recall a time when I was asked what Lutherans believe. I began by saying we believe in the triune God, one God in three persons. I got no further. My questioner became upset and vehemently insisted that the Holy Spirit isn't a person. "He's a spirit; Jesus was the only one who became a person," he argued. The term *person* obviously meant something different to that man than it did to me. To him a person is a human being with flesh and bones. I certainly know that Jesus Christ is the only member of the Trinity who became human and lived among us for a while. When I referred to the Father and the Holy Spirit as "persons," I meant something else.

The Augsburg Confession explains what Lutherans mean: "The word 'person' is to be understood as the Fathers employed the term in this connection, not as a part or a property of another but as that which exists of itself."[5] A person is a separate being, one who can speak, hear, think, will, and act. Calling the Holy Spirit a person, therefore, means to say that he is a real and separate personality, a living being who is distinguishable from any other being.

A *distinct person*

The Bible teaches that the Holy Spirit is a distinct person in the triune God. The passages that mention him with the Father and Son are the most obvious scriptural evidence of that. When the Spirit is placed on the same level or coordinated in a series with the Father and Son, whose personalities are unquestioned, this clearly shows he is a personal being also. Jesus set the Holy Spirit alongside the Father and the Son when he commanded us, "Go and make disciples of all nations, baptizing them in the name of the Father and of the Son and of the Holy Spirit" (Matthew 28:19). The apostle Peter clearly identifies three persons at work in the believers "who have been chosen according to the foreknowledge of God the Father, through the sanctifying work of the Spirit, for obedience to Jesus Christ" (1 Peter 1:2).

Numerous verses in Scripture mention all three members of the triune God. These verses would be nonsense if the three weren't separate and distinct from one another. At Jesus' baptism, as he went up out of the water, "heaven was opened, and he saw the Spirit of God descending like a dove and lighting on him. And a voice from heaven said, 'This is my Son, whom I love; with him I am well pleased'" (Matthew 3:16,17). Jesus provided another example when he told his disciples he would send the Holy Spirit, who would come from the Father: "When the Counselor comes, whom I will send to you from the Father, the Spirit of truth who goes out from the Father, he will testify about me" (John 15:26). Another passage that clearly identifies all three persons says: "God anointed Jesus of Nazareth with the Holy Spirit" (Acts 10:38).

The many personal activities ascribed to the Holy Spirit also demonstrate that he is a distinct person. The Spirit gives spiritual gifts to believers (1 Corinthians 12:11). He grieves (Ephesians 4:30). He "testifies" (Romans 8:16), "calls out" (Galatians 4:6), "helps us . . . intercedes for us" (Romans 8:26), and teaches (1 Corinthians 2:13). Jesus says the Holy Spirit will come, convict, guide, speak, hear, and tell (John 16:7-13). Verses such as these would be absurd if the Holy Spirit weren't a distinct being who could do the things he is described as doing.

In the early Christian church some denied the biblical truth that God is three distinct persons. Some false teachers advocated *modal monarchianism*, the teaching that only one person in God reveals himself in three different modes, or forms, of activity. In other words, the Father, the Son, and the Holy Spirit are merely three roles, or parts, played by one divine being. According to this false doctrine, God is like an actor in a drama who changes costumes between scenes to play different characters. An illustration is sometimes used today that reflects the same misunderstanding. The Trinity is likened to a man who is at the same time a son to his parents, a husband to his wife, and a father to his children. This illustration is flawed because it pictures only one person doing three different jobs. No one would ever speak of that man as if he were three distinct human persons. But Father, Son, and Holy Spirit are three distinct divine persons.

A variation of this false teaching is called *dynamic monarchianism*. It maintains that the Holy Spirit is only a divine power coming from God and at work in humans (*dynamis* is the Greek word for "power"). According to this false teaching, the Holy Spirit is not a distinct being at all, but a force that emanates from God and overtakes a person. The term *Holy Spirit*, therefore, merely personifies

God's influence or power. In other words, it says Scripture is using picture language so simpleminded humans can understand that God is at work in them.

A modern-day form of monarchianism claims the Holy Spirit is really the risen Christ invisibly present and at work in the church. One far-out theory even sees the working of the Holy Spirit as the fulfillment of Jesus' promise to come again. Oral Roberts gives us an example of this form of monarchianism when he writes: "The Holy Spirit is Christ come back in His own invisible, unlimited form. . . . As an example let's take water. It can manifest itself in three ways; as liquid, as ice, as vapor. But it is still water."[6] We need look no further than Jesus' calling the Holy Spirit "another Counselor" (John 14:16) to realize that Jesus and the Spirit cannot be the same person.

Monarchianism is a fancy name for unitarianism, which denies the Trinity. The Bible passages we have discussed show that any denial of the distinct personality of the Holy Spirit violates God's revealed truth.

Equal to Father and Son

The Holy Spirit truly is a divine person, distinct from the Father and the Son. Scripture also teaches that he is their equal. In the Bible we find the Spirit listed regularly with the other two members of the Trinity as a third and equal partner. We never see any indication that he is inferior in any way.

Consider a couple Old Testament examples. In Isaiah 42 God the Father speaks in verses that refer to Jesus, the Christ. The Father says, "Here is my servant, whom I uphold, my chosen one in whom I delight; I will put my Spirit on him and he will bring justice to the nations" (verse 1). In Isaiah 48:16, Christ is speaking with clear ref-

erence to the Father and the Spirit: "Now the Sovereign
LORD has sent me, with his Spirit."

In the New Testament we need look no further than
Jesus' command to baptize "in the name of the Father and
of the Son and of the Holy Spirit" (Matthew 28:19). It
treats the Holy Spirit as an equal of the other two persons.
Numerous other New Testament passages illustrate the
same truth. Jesus showed the intertwining of three equals
when he promised, "The Counselor, the Holy Spirit,
whom the Father will send in my name, will teach you all
things and will remind you of everything I have said to
you" (John 14:26).

Three familiar passages from the writings of Saint Paul
also illustrate this intertwining of equal partners.

> When the time had fully come, God sent his Son . . . that
> we might receive the full rights of sons. Because you are
> sons, God sent the Spirit of his Son into our hearts, the
> Spirit who calls out, "*Abba*, Father." (Galatians 4:4-6)

> Through him [Jesus] we both have access to the Father by
> one Spirit. (Ephesians 2:18)

> May the grace of the Lord Jesus Christ, and the love of
> God, and the fellowship of the Holy Spirit be with you all.
> (2 Corinthians 13:14)

The apostolic blessing is familiar to us. It is very significant that when Paul places a blessing from God on people,
he speaks of the blessing coming from three distinct persons in God.

If the passages we just studied are not sufficient to con-
vince people that the Spirit is equal to the Father and the
Son, the Bible gives irrefutable proof by calling the Holy
Spirit God. Ananias and Sapphira attempted to deceive

the early church and pull a fast one on the Lord. They lied about a gift they had presented to the apostles. Peter confronted them: "Ananias, how is it that Satan has so filled your heart that you have lied to the Holy Spirit . . . ? You have not lied to men but to God" (Acts 5:3,4).

In later chapters of this book, we will study the Holy Spirit's divine names, his divine attributes, his divine works, and the divine honor we owe him. These chapters will reinforce our conviction that the Holy Spirit is in every way equal to the Father and the Son.

Perhaps a word should be mentioned here about one New Testament passage that was sometimes used in the past to prove the equality of the three persons of the Trinity— 1 John 5:7,8: "For there are three that testify in heaven: the Father, the Word and the Holy Spirit, and these three are one" (NIV footnote). The Latin Vulgate translation of the Bible contains this verse, but none of the Greek manuscripts of the New Testament contain it. This lack of sound textual evidence has led Bible scholars to conclude that this verse was inserted by a translator or copyist at a later time. Even without this later insertion in 1 John, however, the scriptural evidence for the equality of the Spirit with the Father and the Son is incontestable.

Full God

Martin Luther wrote, "Of these Persons each one is the *entire* God."[7] In the triune God, each person possesses the Godhead fully. In other words, each is full God, not one-third God. Divinity cannot be divided. The Bible states, "There is no God but one" (1 Corinthians 8:4). There are not three Gods and not three one-third Gods who combine to equal one God. Just as the Scriptures teach that "in Christ all the fullness of the Deity lives in bodily form"

(Colossians 2:9), so they also teach that the Holy Spirit is full God.

The Scriptures never divide God's attributes such as omnipotence, omniscience, or omnipresence. The Father does not possess a one-third portion of omnipotence, with the Son holding the second third and the Holy Spirit the last third. It is unscriptural to visualize the three persons of the Godhead pooling their shares to get full almighty power. Nor do the persons possess different abilities. It is against Scripture, for example, to imagine that the Father is the omnipotent one, the Son the omniscient one, and the Holy Spirit the omnipresent one. On the contrary, the Bible ascribes all divine attributes fully and equally to each person. The Holy Spirit, for example, is omnipresent: "Where can I go from your Spirit? Where can I flee from your presence? If I go up to the heavens, you are there; if I make my bed in the depths, you are there" (Psalm 139:7,8).

Divine works and honor also belong fully and equally to each person. In chapter 3 of this book, for example, we will see that Scripture attributes the work of creation to the Holy Spirit as well as to the Father and to the Son.

The Old Testament prophets received their messages from the LORD: "I will listen to what God the LORD will say" (Psalm 85:8). In the New Testament, this LORD who spoke is identified as the Holy Spirit: "Prophecy never had its origin in the will of man, but men spoke from God as they were carried along by the Holy Spirit" (2 Peter 1:21). The Holy Spirit is identified with the LORD, for he is full God.

Familiar illustrations picture the triune God. One is a triangle with three equal sides. It takes all three sides to form one triangle. Another illustration is a shamrock with three equally sized leaves. It takes three leaves to make one shamrock. Then there's the word *God*; three letters are needed to spell *God*. Take away any one letter, and you don't have *God* anymore. These illustrations are a bit misleading, however. One side alone is not a triangle; one leaf alone is not a shamrock; one letter alone is not *God*. But each person of the Trinity—Father, Son, and Holy Spirit—is God! Each by himself is full God!

How can three distinct persons each be full God? How can three "full Gods" be only one God? These are mysteries of the Trinity—mysteries within the wonder of God. Luther stated the situation clearly: "Reason cannot comprehend that one thing contains no distinctions and at the same time is three distinct things."[8] Scripture nowhere offers an explanation. It emphasizes both unity and plurality and never even hints at the mathematical problem such trinity in unity presents. The Bible merely states the facts.

We need to cultivate the attitude of young Samuel, who said simply, "Speak, for your servant is listening" (1 Samuel 3:10). It is not our task to solve what God does not regard as a problem. Danger lurks when we try to reconcile to human reason what God has not chosen to explain. For the present, we must be content to accept what the Bible says. A day is coming when "we shall see him as he is" (1 John 3:2).

Proceeding from Father and Son

The Father, Son, and Holy Spirit are each full and equal persons of the Godhead. Within that Godhead there is, however, a peculiar relationship of the Holy Spirit to the other two persons. This the Bible describes as *procession*. Jesus speaks of the Holy Spirit as "the Spirit of your Father" (Matthew 10:20). Both Peter and Paul refer to him as "the Spirit of Christ" (Romans 8:9; 1 Peter 1:11). Jesus tells us: "[The Spirit] will not speak on his own. . . . He will bring glory to me by taking from what is mine and making it known to you" (John 16:13,14).

The relationship that makes the names "Spirit of your Father" and "Spirit of Christ" true is described by Jesus this way: "When the Counselor comes, whom I will send to you from the Father, the Spirit of truth who goes out [KJV: proceedeth] from the Father, he will testify about me" (John 15:26). The Holy Spirit proceeds from the Father; he is sent by Jesus. The Athanasian Creed expresses that truth in these words: "The Holy Spirit is neither made nor created nor begotten, but proceeds from the Father and the Son" (*Christian Worship* [CW] page 132).

This procession from the Father and the Son is understood as an eternal procession. It is not just a matter of the Father and the Son sending the Holy Spirit onto the New Testament church at Pentecost. Somehow, in a way that goes beyond our comprehension, the Spirit proceeded from the Father and the Son from all eternity, just as the Son was begotten of the Father from all eternity.

Some may argue that since the Holy Spirit comes from the Father and the Son, he must be inferior to them. Everyday experience exposes the faulty logic of such a claim, however. Human children are not necessarily inferior to their parents. Many children equal or even exceed their parents in things such as size, intelligence, skills, or accomplishments. Within the Trinity, procession does not mean inferiority in any way. The Holy Spirit is full God. He is eternal. Procession, therefore, is something unexplainable that occurs within the equal persons of the mysterious Trinity. The Scriptures give us no further details.

The doctrine of procession led to heated debate in the early Christian church. The Eastern, or Greek-speaking, part of the early church confessed in the original version of the Nicene Creed (A.D. 325) that the Holy Spirit proceeds from the Father with no mention of him proceeding also from the Son. Saint Augustine later called attention to the many Scripture verses that point to the Holy Spirit coming from or being sent by the Son (A.D. 400). At a church council in Toledo, Spain, in A.D. 589, the Western, or Latin-speaking, church amended the Nicene Creed to read, "who proceeds from the Father *and the Son*." This brought about the *Filioque* (Latin for "and from the Son") Controversy. The easterners charged that a false doctrine was inserted into the Nicene Creed by this unauthorized addition. This *Filioque* Controversy was one of the factors that led to the Great Schism of 1054. The pope in Rome excommunicated the Eastern church. In turn, the patriarch of Constantinople excommunicated the pope. The Christian church was split into the Orthodox churches of Asia and the Roman Catholic Church of Europe. The *Filioque* Controversy remains an unresolved issue between those churches to the present day.

It may be debatable whether the Western church had the right on its own to alter the Nicene Creed. What cannot be debated is the correctness of defending the deity of the Holy Spirit and his equality within the Trinity. It is false doctrine to teach that the Holy Spirit is subordinate or inferior to the Father or the Son. While the Holy Spirit usually is placed third in a series, this is simply a logical sequence. The Apostles' Creed would be just as correct if it began with "I believe in the Holy Spirit" and ended with "I believe in God, the Father almighty." Such a reversal would not follow as logically as the traditional order, however. When we speak of the Holy Spirit as "the third person in the Trinity," we are simply using the numerical listing found in passages such as the Great Commission (Matthew 28:19). It would be wrong to read into that term any implication of lower rank or less dignity.

Some might still ask, "What difference does it make whether we are clear regarding the person of the Holy Spirit?" That question is easy to answer. In the First Commandment the Lord says, "You shall have no other gods." Believers desire to obey their Lord. Therefore, we need to know who the true God is, the one we are to fear, love, and trust above all things. It would be sinful to worship or revere the Holy Spirit as God if he were not God. On the other hand, if the Holy Spirit is God, as the Bible teaches, then we are sinning if we slight him or withhold from him the honor he is due.

2

His Divine Names and Attributes

The Holy Spirit is God. His divinity is shown by the fact that he is given names that could be true only if he were God. Moreover, according to the Bible, the Holy Spirit has attributes (that is, qualities or traits) that only God could have.

His divine names

In biblical times names were chosen for their meaning. For example, Abram's name was changed to Abraham ("father of many"). Think of the names Isaac ("he laughs"), Esau ("hairy"), and Jacob ("he grabs the heel") or the beautiful names for our Lord Jesus: Jesus ("Savior"), Christ ("the Anointed One"), and Immanuel[9] ("God with us"). In the same way, the names for the Holy Spirit are descriptive titles more than proper names. They are filled with meaning, telling us about him and his work.

The third person of the Trinity is called the *Holy Spirit* or the *Holy Ghost*. While the first of the two is more in vogue these days, Holy Spirit and Holy Ghost are interchangeable translations without any intended difference in meaning. Both teach that the Holy Spirit is a real being, but one who is not confined to a particular place or trapped in a physical body.

Spirit and *ghost* are translations of the Hebrew word *ruach* and the Greek word *pneuma*. Literally these words mean "breath" or "wind." The picture of the Holy Spirit as breath is brought out in John 20:22: Jesus "breathed on them and said, 'Receive the Holy Spirit.'" The Spirit is the outbreathing of God. He is life going forth from God in a personal form to give us life. When the Holy Spirit is in our hearts, the life and breath of God himself dwells in us. Paul uses this same picture for the Holy Spirit at work when he writes, "All Scripture is God-breathed" (2 Timothy 3:16). Read Ezekiel 37:1-14 for an expanded example of the Holy Spirit as the breath of God's mouth, breathing life into spiritually dry bones.

Jesus also pictures the Holy Spirit as wind: "The wind blows wherever it pleases. You hear its sound, but you cannot tell where it comes from or where it is going. So it is with everyone born of the Spirit" (John 3:8). In this verse the same Greek word (*pneuma*) is translated "wind" and then "Spirit."

The name *wind* as applied to the Holy Spirit (Holy Wind) is rich in significance. Like the wind, the Holy Spirit is sovereign. You cannot dictate to the wind. It does as it wills. In the same way, we cannot dictate to the Spirit.

"He gives them [his gifts] to each one, just as he determines" (1 Corinthians 12:11). Like the wind, the Spirit is invisible, but nonetheless perceptible and real. We don't see the wind, but we see its effects. No one questions the reality of the wind, for we can see dust and leaves blowing; we can see a sailboat driven along by it. In a similar way, although we cannot see the Spirit, we cannot question his existence, for where he is at work, spiritually dead sinners are brought to faith—they are given new life—and become new creatures. Like the wind, the Holy Spirit is powerful. Consider the awesome power of a tornado or hurricane. In the same way the Spirit's power breaks the hold of sin and Satan and brings us into the kingdom of God.

Perhaps you have wondered if the Holy Spirit is a *he* or an *it*? Christian literature can be a little confusing on this point because both *he* and *it* are used of the Spirit. In the original Greek of the New Testament, the word *pneuma* is a neuter noun and so, according to rules of Greek grammar, takes the neuter pronoun *it*. When translating into English, however, the masculine pronoun *he* is the better choice to show that the Holy Spirit is a real and personal being, not just an impersonal force.

The descriptive word *holy* is frequently added to the Spirit's name. *Holy* means "perfect and without sin." More than that, it means "separated from things common or profane and consecrated for sacred service." As part of the Trinity, the Holy Spirit is set aside for divine service.

Another significant name for the Holy Spirit is *Paraclete*. This name is a Greek word taken over into English. Before Jesus left this world, he promised his disciples, "I will ask the Father, and he will give you another Counselor [*Paraclete*] to be with you forever—the Spirit of truth" (John 14:16,17). *Paraclete* is usually translated "counselor" or "comforter." It means much more than that, however. It means "a person who is called or summoned to one's side." In classical Greek, a *paraclete* was a defense attorney in a trial. In later Greek, *paraclete* referred to anyone who takes another's side, pleads his cause, and speaks a good word for him.

The Paraclete is the one who remains at our side to help us. For the disciples Jesus had been such a paraclete. After Jesus' ascension the Holy Spirit took Jesus' place at the believers' side. The Spirit comforts us, guides us, and protects us. "Counselor" is a good translation for *paraclete*. "Helper," "sustainer," "vindicator," "adviser," "protector," and "prompter" are other translations that would work just as well.

The Holy Spirit is our "stand-byer" or our "part-taker." He stands near, ready to offer help in any need. The truth that the Spirit is the ever-present Paraclete banishes fear. How can we be afraid in the face of any peril if God is by our side to help us and to take up our defense?

His descriptive titles

The Scriptures use many other descriptive titles to tell us about the Holy Spirit and his work.

He is called *the Spirit of truth* (John 14:17). This title means that beyond being truthful and deceiving no one, the Holy Spirit is the embodiment of divine truth. He brings it, reveals it, and causes it to become effective in our lives. "When he, the Spirit of truth, comes, he will guide you into all truth," Jesus promises (John 16:13). Only through the Holy Spirit's teaching do we come to know God's truth.

The Spirit of holiness is another descriptive title the Bible uses (Romans 1:4). At first glance this title may seem to say nothing more than the name Holy Spirit already tells us. But there is a difference. The name Holy Spirit empha- sizes that the Spirit's character is holy. On the other hand, the title *Spirit of holiness* brings out the thought that he imparts holiness to others. He makes us holy, cleansed of our sin and set aside for God's service.

This same thing applies to other titles given to the Holy Spirit. He is called *the Spirit of life* (Romans 8:2). He sets us free from the law that leads to sin and death. In turn, he imparts spiritual life and victory. He is *the Spirit of grace* (Hebrews 10:29). Only by the work of the Spirit in our hearts do we receive the grace, the undeserved love, that God has for us in Jesus Christ. The Holy Spirit is *the Spirit of glory* (1 Peter 4:14). When we face reproach for Christ's sake, we can rejoice, for the Spirit holds before our eyes the glory that awaits us. "The Spirit him- self testifies with our spirit that we are God's children. Now if we are children, then we are heirs—heirs of God and co-heirs with Christ, if indeed we share in his suffer- ings in order that we may also share in his glory" (Romans 8:16,17).

The Scriptures love to pile up descriptive titles for the Holy Spirit. Isaiah 11:2 is an excellent example of that: "The Spirit of the LORD will rest on him [the Messiah]— the Spirit of wisdom and of understanding, the Spirit of counsel and of power, the Spirit of knowledge and of the fear of the LORD."

The verse just quoted illustrates a difficulty in under- standing the descriptive titles for the Holy Spirit. Does "the Spirit of wisdom and of understanding," for example, refer to the Holy Spirit, or is it referring to a quality (a "spirit") within the coming Messiah? In other words, does Isaiah mean the Holy Spirit with his wisdom and understanding will be in Jesus? Or does Isaiah mean to say that the Messiah will be a man full of wisdom and understanding? The question is, Does Isaiah mean *Spirit* (capitalized *S*) or *spirit* (lowercased *s*)? We should realize that the capital letters are not part of the inspired manuscripts of the Bible, but are interpretations by the translators.

Let me give you an example where both the King James Version (KJV) and the New International Version (NIV) seem to have made the wrong choice. The NIV translates Numbers 27:18 this way: "The LORD said to Moses, 'Take Joshua son of Nun, a man in whom is the spirit, and lay your hand on him.'" The KJV also leaves "spirit" lowercased. The lowercased "spirit" makes no sense in this verse, however. What kind of spirit does Joshua have? a team spirit? a humble spirit? a spirit of leadership? In this instance the capitalized "Spirit" clearly fits the line of thought. "Spirit," capitalized, would be telling us Joshua was a man empowered by the Holy Spirit and so obviously a good choice to succeed Moses. Such indwelling by the Holy Spirit is clearly taught in Scripture. For example, "I will put my Spirit in you and move you to follow my decrees" (Ezekiel 36:27).

As you read the Bible, notice whether the word *spirit* is capitalized or lowercased. That will help you understand how the translators interpret the verse. Don't just accept the translators' decision, however. Discerning readers will need to search for themselves whether *Spirit* or *spirit* is meant. The Holy Spirit working through the Word is there to help us understand correctly. Fortunately, in many cases the truth remains the same whether the s is capitalized or not, since the Holy Spirit must produce any God-pleasing spirit in us.

Another especially comforting title for the Holy Spirit is found in Ephesians 1:13,14: "Having believed, you were marked in him with a seal, the promised Holy Spirit, who is a *deposit* guaranteeing our inheritance until the redemption of those who are God's possession." The Holy Spirit in our heart is a deposit, or a down payment, guaranteeing eternal life. The picture is familiar to people in our modern world who frequently buy on an installment plan. A down payment is a pledge that the balance due will be paid in full later. In the spiritual realm the Holy Spirit is God's pledge assuring that full payment of all God's promises will follow. Paul uses this same comforting description for the Holy Spirit in 2 Corinthians 1:22: God "set his seal of ownership on us, and put his Spirit in our hearts as a deposit, guaranteeing what is to come." When the Holy Spirit entered our hearts, he brought us to faith, which grabbed hold of the truth that Christ rescued us from our sins. Now the Holy Spirit in us guarantees that when the time is right, God will rescue us from all evil. Even our dead bodies will be rescued for eternal glory.

What do these beautiful names for the Holy Spirit mean for us? Each name forms additional evidence that the Holy Spirit is God. Only the true God could have such names and be the embodiment of such qualities. There is never need for us to doubt. Our faith rests in the one true God. The Bible proves that over and over again. Even more, we know that this powerful God stays by our side throughout our lives and guarantees us an eternal inheritance in heaven. The Holy Spirit—God's Breath, God's Wind in us—is our Paraclete and the deposit guaranteeing our future of eternal life with him together with the Father and the Son.

Divine attributes

The Scriptures not only call the Holy Spirit by divine names, but they also ascribe to him attributes that belong to God only. The Bible reveals that the Holy Spirit possesses the same divine traits and qualities as do the Father and the Son.

The Holy Spirit is "the eternal Spirit" (Hebrews 9:14). Only God is eternal, without beginning, without end.

Psalm 139:7,8 asks: "Where can I go from your Spirit? Where can I flee from your presence? If I go up to the heavens, you are there; if I make my bed in the depths, you are there." Here the divine attribute of omnipresence is ascribed to the Holy Spirit. He is present everywhere. God in no way is bound by the limitations of time and space. This divine attribute contains a word of warning for us. There is no place where God does not see us. Nothing is hidden from him. On the other hand, omnipresence is an especially consoling quality in the case of the Holy Spirit. No place or space can separate us from the Spirit's loving presence. We need fear no evil even in the darkest valleys of life. Psalm 139 draws that conclusion too: "If I rise on the wings of the dawn, if I settle on the far side of the sea, even there your hand will guide me, your right hand will hold me fast" (verses 9,10).

"There are different kinds of gifts, but the same Spirit. There are different kinds of service, but the same Lord. All these are the work of one and the same Spirit, and he gives them to each one, just as he determines" (1 Corinthians 12:4,5,11). These verses tell us the Holy Spirit has almighty power, for none but God possesses the power to bestow spiritual gifts as he pleases. The Spirit is omnipotent; his power knows no limits.

"The Spirit searches all things, even the deep things of God. For who among men knows the thoughts of a man except the man's spirit within him? In the same way no one knows the thoughts of God except the Spirit of God" (1 Corinthians 2:10,11). These verses tell us the Holy Spirit possesses the divine attribute of omniscience. He knows all things, even the deep mysteries of God.

The Bible tells us of other divine qualities the Spirit possesses. He is "the Spirit of glory" (1 Peter 4:14), "the Spirit of grace" (Hebrews 10:29), and God's "good Spirit" (Nehemiah 9:20). Paul cites his trait of love (Romans 15:30).

What does it mean for us that the Holy Spirit possesses divine attributes? It means he has the ability to complete all the important tasks he has been given to do in our lives! Moreover, he has the faithfulness to carry through his saving work to the very end. In the next two chapters we will study examples of the Spirit's many divine works in the Old and New Testaments.

3

His Work in Old Testament Times

Before Jesus left his disciples, he promised them and us, "The Father . . . will give you another Counselor to be with you forever—[namely] the Spirit of truth" (John 14:16,17). A brief glimpse at Old Testament history shows why this is such an exciting promise, one meant to comfort all believers.

Active in the beginning

Already on the first day of world history, we find the Holy Spirit at work. "Now the earth was formless and empty, darkness was over the surface of the deep, and the Spirit of God was hovering over the waters" (Genesis 1:2). Together with the Father and the Son, the Holy Spirit

31

created all things, including humans. God said, "Let us make man in our image, in our likeness" (verse 26). Elsewhere Scripture confirms the Spirit's role in the work of creation. "The Spirit of God has made me; the breath of the Almighty gives me life" (Job 33:4). The one true God created the universe; the Holy Spirit played an active part.

In the earliest period of this world's existence, the Holy Spirit worked to keep God's creatures close to their Lord. It was a frustrating struggle. The godly intermarried with the godless and followed their sinful and rebellious ways. God warned that the Holy Spirit would not struggle with the wicked indefinitely. "Then the LORD said, 'My Spirit will not contend with man forever, for he is mortal; his days will be a hundred and twenty years'" (Genesis 6:3). After those 120 years, God brought that ungodly age to an end by the flood.

At the time of Moses

The Holy Spirit continued to make his presence felt as he directed the history of God's chosen people, the Israelites. The Bible shows the Holy Spirit at work at the time of the exodus from Egypt. At Mount Sinai God revealed in detail his desires for the tabernacle. "Then the LORD said to Moses, 'See, I have chosen Bezalel son of Uri, the son of Hur, of the tribe of Judah, and I have filled him with the Spirit of God, with skill, ability and knowledge in all kinds of crafts—to make artistic designs for work in gold, silver and bronze, to cut and set stones, to work in wood, and to engage in all kinds of craftsmanship" (Exodus 31:1-5). God gave Bezalel the skills needed to execute the plans. The Holy Spirit at work in Bezalel gave him willingness to undertake the project and faithfulness to carry it to completion.

The Lord provided faithful leaders for his people. Moses was equipped for his task by the indwelling of the Holy Spirit. But Moses was not alone. The Holy Spirit empowered 70 elders to assist Moses in leading the people. He gave them a special gift to confirm that he was with them. "Then the LORD came down in the cloud and spoke with him [Moses], and he took of the Spirit that was on him [Moses] and put the Spirit on the seventy elders. When the Spirit rested on them, they prophesied" (Numbers 11:25).

Seven hundred years later the prophet Isaiah would look back at the Exodus. On the one hand, Isaiah saw the sin that resulted in 40 years of wilderness wandering. "They rebelled and grieved his Holy Spirit. So he turned and became their enemy and he himself fought against them" (Isaiah 63:10). On the other hand, Isaiah saw the grace of God, who kept his Holy Spirit at work in the people. He "set his Holy Spirit among them. . . . They were given rest by the Spirit of the LORD. This is how you guided your people to make for yourself a glorious name" (verses 11,14).

After 40 years of wandering, it was time for the Israelites to enter the Promised Land. Moses was not permitted to go any farther. But the Holy Spirit did not leave the nation without a faithful leader at this crucial time. "So the LORD said to Moses, 'Take Joshua son of Nun, a man in whom is the [Spirit], and lay your hand on him. Have him stand before Eleazar the priest and the entire assembly and commission him in their presence'" (Numbers 27:18,19).

During the time of the judges
Joshua died after a lifetime of faithful service. The Israelites then entered into a new relationship of special dependence on the Lord. God gave them no head of

government to lead them and no standing army to defend them. When enemies came to oppress the nation, the people needed to trust the Lord and wait for him to intervene. God did not fail them! In every time of crisis, the Holy Spirit commissioned a leader, called a judge. Then the Spirit gave the judge the wisdom, skill, and courage necessary to drive off the enemy.

As was to become a tragic habit, the Israelites did evil and forgot the Lord. At one such time God, therefore, gave them into the hands of the king of Aram. The people got the message and pleaded for God's forgiveness. The Holy Spirit heard their cry and raised up Othniel to be their deliverer. "The Spirit of the LORD came upon him, so that he became Israel's judge and went to war. The LORD gave Cushan-Rishathaim king of Aram into the hands of Othniel, who overpowered him. So the land had peace for forty years, until Othniel son of Kenaz died" (Judges 3:10,11).

Gideon was another such leader. "Now all the Midianites, Amalekites and other eastern peoples joined forces and crossed over the Jordan and camped in the Valley of Jezreel. Then the Spirit of the LORD came upon Gideon, and he blew a trumpet, summoning the Abiezrites to follow him. He sent messengers throughout Manasseh, calling them to arms" (Judges 6:33-35). Gideon would not need all the men who answered his call. God gave him the victory by means of three hundred men armed with trumpets, torches, and empty pitchers.

The judge Samson is an intriguing illustration of what the Holy Spirit can accomplish through sinful humans. Samson certainly had his flaws. He was a skirt-chasing loner who made one unwise decision after another. Yet for 20 years the Holy Spirit used him single-handedly to keep the Philistines at bay and the Israelites at peace.

The Holy Spirit called Samson for God's service: "The Spirit of the LORD began to stir him" (Judges 13:25). The Holy Spirit gave him the gift of supernatural power: "The Spirit of the LORD came upon him in power so that he tore the lion apart with his bare hands as he might have torn a young goat" (14:6). The Spirit used that power against the Philistine enemies of Israel: "Then the Spirit of the LORD came upon him in power. He went down to Ashkelon, [and] struck down thirty of their men" (verse 19). "As he approached Lehi, the Philistines came toward him shouting. The Spirit of the LORD came upon him in power. The ropes on his arms became like charred flax, and the bindings dropped from his hands. Finding a fresh jawbone of a donkey, he grabbed it and struck down a thousand men" (15:14,15).

During the time of the kings

The people were not satisfied with God's arrangement under the judges. In weakness of faith they craved the security they felt a king would afford. The judge Samuel was sent to anoint Saul and assure him that the Holy Spirit would equip him for the kingship. Samuel prophesied to Saul: "You will meet a procession of prophets. . . . The Spirit of the LORD will come upon you in power, and you will prophesy with them; and you will be changed into a different person" (1 Samuel 10:5,6). All happened just as Samuel had said: "God changed Saul's heart, and all these signs were fulfilled that day" (verse 9).

The Spirit guided the young king in his first crisis. He led Saul to act quickly and decisively to save the besieged city of Jabesh Gilead. "When Saul heard their words, the Spirit of God came upon him in power, and he burned with anger. He took a pair of oxen, cut them into pieces,

and sent the pieces by messengers throughout Israel, pro-
claiming, 'This is what will be done to the oxen of anyone
who does not follow Saul and Samuel'" (1 Samuel 11:6,7).
Saul rescued Jabesh Gilead, saving its men from having
their right eyes gouged out by the Ammonites. The grateful and godly King Saul gave the credit where it belonged:
"This day the LORD has rescued Israel" (verse 13). Tragi-
cally, Saul did not remain close to his Lord but rejected
the Holy Spirit's leading. In the end God rejected him as
king. Scripture records this sad fact: "The Spirit of the
LORD had departed from Saul, and an evil spirit from the
LORD tormented him" (16:14).

The Holy Spirit had a much happier time with Israel's
second king, David. "Samuel took the horn of oil and
anointed him in the presence of his brothers, and from
that day on the Spirit of the LORD came upon David in
power" (1 Samuel 16:13). The Holy Spirit played an
active role in the conflict that raged between Saul and
David. Once again, the Spirit chose a supernatural sign to
show where he stood.

> Word came to Saul: "David is in Naioth at Ramah"; so he
> sent men to capture him. But when they saw a group of
> prophets prophesying, with Samuel standing there as their
> leader, the Spirit of God came upon Saul's men and they
> also prophesied. Saul was told about it, and he sent more
> men, and they prophesied too. . . . So Saul went to Naioth
> at Ramah. But the Spirit of God came even upon him,
> and he walked along prophesying until he came to
> Naioth. (19:19-21,23)

We will discuss the Holy Spirit's supernatural signs in
chapter 8. We note at this point, however, that the outpouring of the Holy Spirit in signs and wonders happened

already in the Old Testament when the Spirit wanted to make clear his presence or to emphasize his point.

Speaking his last words, David looked back over his life and writings. He summed them up this way: "The Spirit of the LORD spoke through me; his word was on my tongue" (2 Samuel 23:2).

The great kingdom of David was split into two. Unfaithful kings and sinful people brought destruction for the Northern Kingdom and the Babylonian captivity for the Southern Kingdom. The Holy Spirit brought a remnant home again, however, and saw to it that the temple was rebuilt. Zerubbabel, the exile leader, did not have the might or wealth David and Solomon enjoyed. The Holy Spirit was with him, however, and enabled him to get the job done. "This is the word of the LORD to Zerubbabel: 'Not by might nor by power, but by my Spirit,' says the LORD Almighty" (Zechariah 4:6).

Spoke through the prophets

The Holy Spirit was especially active in Old Testament times as he spoke through the prophets. At the time of Israel's most wicked rulers, King Ahab and Queen Jezebel, the Holy Spirit sent Elijah. God-fearing Obadiah recognized that the Spirit guided the ministry of Elijah. He told Elijah: "I don't know where the Spirit of the LORD may carry you when I leave you" (1 Kings 18:12). Likewise, the prophets of Jericho were certain the Holy Spirit directed Elijah's path. They confessed that certainty when they offered to search for Elijah after he was taken to heaven. They explained: "Perhaps the Spirit of the LORD has picked him up and set him down on some mountain or in some valley" (2 Kings 2:16).

The Spirit's power compelled even the wicked sooth-
sayer Balaam to proclaim God's message. Balak offered
Balaam a handsome fee to come and curse the people of
Israel, but the Holy Spirit had a different idea. God used a
talking donkey to get Balaam's attention and then the
angel of the Lord, with his sword drawn, changed Balaam's
mind. Instead of curses, Balaam delivered the Spirit's message: "When Balaam looked out and saw Israel encamped
tribe by tribe, the Spirit of God came upon him and he
uttered his oracle: . . . 'How beautiful are your tents,
O Jacob, your dwelling places, O Israel! . . . May those
who bless you be blessed and those who curse you be
cursed!'" (Numbers 24:2,3,5,9).

The Holy Spirit granted the prophet Ezekiel extraordinary visions, which, in turn, he proclaimed to the people.
In the vision of the valley of dry bones, the Holy Spirit
showed Ezekiel that he would breathe new life into the
nation of Israel (then in exile). More importantly, in that
vision he promised to breathe new spiritual life into the
spiritually dead of all ages. "Then you, my people, will
know that I am the LORD, when I open your graves and
bring you up from them. I will put my Spirit in you and
you will live, and I will settle you in your own land"
(Ezekiel 37:13,14). There is hope for us also, because the
ultimate fulfillment of this vision comes through Jesus
Christ. God was preserving the Old Testament remnant
so the Messiah could come as promised. That promise
will be fully realized on the Last Day, when Christ gathers
the believers of all ages and lands before God's throne,
there forever to live with the Lord.

The prophets proclaimed God's truth—often at great
personal peril. The Holy Spirit gave them the message and
also the courage to speak. Micah, for example, could look

into the eyes of those who threatened him and say: "'Do not prophesy,' their prophets say. 'Do not prophesy about these things; disgrace will not overtake us.' But as for me, I am filled with power, with the Spirit of the LORD, and with justice and might, to declare to Jacob his transgression, to Israel his sin" (Micah 2:6; 3:8). The Spirit also gave Micah the privilege of sharing this comforting assurance: "Who is a God like you, who pardons sin and forgives the transgression of the remnant of his inheritance? You do not stay angry forever but delight to show mercy. You will again have compassion on us; you will tread our sins underfoot and hurl all our iniquities into the depths of the sea" (7:18,19).

The prophets, emboldened by the Holy Spirit, got the message out. The prophet Zechariah had to give this sad report on the people's response: "They refused to pay attention; stubbornly they turned their backs and stopped up their ears. They made their hearts as hard as flint and would not listen to the law or to the words that the LORD Almighty had sent by his Spirit through the earlier prophets" (Zechariah 7:11,12). That tragic commentary also applies to many in our world today.

The Holy Spirit was at work in Old Testament times in a way that is especially important to us. The Spirit, who called the prophets and spoke through them, also caused those prophets to record their words. Then the Holy Spirit preserved their writings and passed them on to us in the Bible. "No prophecy of Scripture came about by the prophet's own interpretation. For prophecy never had its origin in the will of man, but men spoke from God as they were carried along by the Holy Spirit" (2 Peter 1:20,21).

Told of wonders to come

Under the guidance of the Holy Spirit, the Old Testament writers told of wondrous things to come. They wrote about the coming Messiah, giving numerous details that would be helpful in identifying the Christ when he arrived. Here are a few examples from David's psalms:

> My God, my God, why have you forsaken me? (22:1)

> All who see me mock me; they hurl insults, shaking their heads: "He trusts in the LORD; let the LORD rescue him. Let him deliver him, since he delights in him." (verses 7,8)

> You lay me in the dust of death. Dogs have surrounded me; a band of evil men has encircled me, they have pierced my hands and my feet. (verses 15,16)

> They divide my garments among them and cast lots for my clothing. (verse 18)

> You will not abandon me to the grave, nor will you let your Holy One see decay. (16:10)

The prophets said the Holy Spirit would play an active part in the Savior's work. Consider Isaiah's words: "A shoot will come up from the stump of Jesse; from his roots a Branch will bear fruit. The Spirit of the LORD will rest on him—the Spirit of wisdom and of understanding, the Spirit of counsel and of power, the Spirit of knowledge and of the fear of the LORD" (Isaiah 11:1,2).

The prophets also foretold the Spirit's life-giving work in the people of future ages—us included. Once again Isaiah gives a good taste of what the prophets promised:

> "I will pour out my Spirit on your offspring, and my blessing on your descendants. They will spring up like grass in a meadow, like poplar trees by flowing streams." (44:3,4)

"My Spirit, who is on you, and my words that I have put in your mouth will not depart from your mouth, or from the mouths of your children, or from the mouths of their descendants from this time on and forever," says the LORD. (59:21)

The Old Testament believers waited generations as the Holy Spirit painstakingly carried out God's plan over the centuries. When troubles come, when our faith or spiritual strength is less than we'd like it to be, we too need to wait for the Holy Spirit. Through the prophet Joel, the Lord promised, "I will pour out my Spirit on all people" (Joel 2:28). We can be confident, therefore, that the Holy Spirit wants to come to us and work in us. He wants to give us his guidance and strength. In upcoming chapters we will learn more from the Scripture about how the Holy Spirit brings his help to us.

The Holy Spirit was actively involved in world history during Old Testament times, empowering leaders and working faith in the hearts of all believers. The numerous Bible passages we have cited prove that fact when they mention the Holy Spirit by name. The Hebrew names for God also show that the Holy Spirit was involved in everything God did. *Adonai*, translated "Lord," and *Elohim*, translated "God," are plural forms that take a singular verb. This grammatical oddity in the Old Testament illustrates the fact of the Trinity. Whenever God acted, the Holy Spirit was involved.

The Old Testament gives a clear, well-documented look at the Holy Spirit's work. It is work he continues to do to this day. Even if we had only the Old Testament, our interest in the Holy Spirit would be aroused. We would be excited about what he can do and eager to claim his blessings for our lives.

4

His Work in the New Testament

The Holy Spirit was very active in Old Testament days, working in the lives of God's people and giving clear testimony to the coming Savior. His presence would become even more apparent in the New Testament as the triune God carried out the plan of salvation. Throughout the New Testament age, the Holy Spirit continued to follow his usual method of operation, however. His goal was not to draw attention to himself, but to testify about Jesus and focus people's attention on him. Jesus told us to expect that of the Spirit: "He will bring glory to me by taking from what is mine and making it known to you" (John 16:14).

His work during Jesus' lifetime

The Holy Spirit brought Old Testament prophecy to a close with Malachi's promise of another great prophet like Elijah, who would prepare the way before the coming Savior. When the time was right according to God's plan, the Holy Spirit fulfilled that prophecy and set in motion the coming of the Messiah.

John the Baptist was that prophet "in the spirit and power of Elijah" (Luke 1:17). Just as the Holy Spirit had guided the life and filled the lips of the first Elijah, so the second Elijah was "filled with the Holy Spirit even from birth" (verse 15). John's ministry was backed by the Spirit's power, so "many of the people of Israel will he bring back to the Lord their God. And he will go on before the Lord . . . to make ready a people prepared for the Lord" (verses 16,17).

The Spirit filled John's parents so they understood and prophesied of the importance of their son and Mary's son.

Elizabeth was filled with the Holy Spirit. "In a loud voice she exclaimed [to Mary]: 'Blessed are you among women, and blessed is the child you will bear!'" (Luke 1:41,42).

Zechariah "was filled with the Holy Spirit and prophesied: 'Praise be to the Lord, the God of Israel, because he has come and has redeemed his people. He has raised up a horn of salvation for us'" (Luke 1:67-69).

The Holy Spirit played an instrumental role also in Jesus' conception and birth. Within the mysterious ways of God, the Holy Spirit was the Trinity's instrument to bring about the conception of God's Son in the virgin Mary. The angel explained to Mary: "The Holy Spirit will come upon you, and the power of the Most High will overshadow you. So the holy one to be born will be called the Son of God" (Luke 1:35). A puzzled Joseph was given the same explanation: "What is conceived in her is from the Holy Spirit. She will give birth to a son, and you are to give him the name Jesus, because he will save his people from their sins" (Matthew 1:20,21).

The Holy Spirit made sure that clear testimony to the Christ Child was given in the temple in Jerusalem. Simeon "was waiting for the consolation of Israel, and the Holy Spirit was upon him. It had been revealed to him by the Holy Spirit that he would not die before he had seen the Lord's Christ. Moved by the Spirit, he went into the temple courts" (Luke 2:25-27). There the Spirit pointed out the baby Jesus. The baby was a seemingly ordinary child from obviously poor parents, yet Simeon saw in him the world's salvation. The Holy Spirit led Simeon to take the child in his arms and boldly testify regarding him, "My eyes have seen your salvation, which you have prepared in the sight of all people, a light for revelation to the Gentiles and for glory to your people Israel" (verses 30-32).

When the time came for Jesus' public ministry to begin, the Holy Spirit was right there. In fact, the Holy Spirit gave the first public testimony that Jesus was the Christ. "As soon as Jesus was baptized, he went up out of the water. At that moment heaven was opened, and he saw the Spirit of God descending like a dove and lighting on him" (Matthew 3:16). That signal by the Holy Spirit was what John the Baptist needed to make his positive identification: "I saw the Spirit come down from heaven as a dove and remain on him. I would not have known him, except that the one who sent me to baptize with water told me, 'The man on whom you see the Spirit come down and remain is he who will baptize with the Holy Spirit.' I have seen and I testify that this is the Son of God" (John

1:32-34). To this day, the dove represents the Holy Spirit in church symbolism.

After Jesus' baptism, the Holy Spirit led Jesus into the wilderness to begin in earnest the battle with Satan. The Paraclete was at Jesus' side to fill him with the power needed in the struggle. "Jesus, full of the Holy Spirit, returned from the Jordan and was led by the Spirit in the desert, where for forty days he was tempted by the devil" (Luke 4:1,2). Jesus beat back Satan's temptations by quoting Old Testament verses, which the Holy Spirit had inspired.

Jesus used words the Holy Spirit had spoken through prophets to confirm that he was the long-awaited Savior. In Nazareth Jesus quoted the Spirit-breathed words of Isaiah: "The Spirit of the Lord is on me, because he has anointed me to preach good news to the poor" (Luke 4:18). Then Jesus applied those words to himself, saying he was the fulfillment of this scripture.

Jesus acknowledged that the Holy Spirit was at work in his miracles and through them was showing that Jesus' messianic claims were true. "If I drive out demons by the Spirit of God, then the kingdom of God has come upon you" (Matthew 12:28). Peter recalled "how God anointed Jesus of Nazareth with the Holy Spirit and power, and how he went around doing good and healing all who were under the power of the devil, because God was with him" (Acts 10:38).

When the decisive moment arrived on Good Friday and the eternal fate of the world hung in the balance, the Holy Spirit was right there too. Jesus "through the eternal Spirit offered himself unblemished to God" (Hebrews 9:14).

Then on Easter the Holy Spirit was there for our triumphant Savior's resurrection. First Peter 3:18 states, "He

[Jesus] was put to death in the body but made alive by the Spirit." The Spirit's presence in us means we too will share the resurrection victory. "For while we are in this tent, we groan and are burdened, because we do not wish to be unclothed but to be clothed with our heavenly dwelling, so that what is mortal may be swallowed up by life. Now it is God who has made us for this very purpose and has given us the Spirit as a deposit, guaranteeing what is to come" (2 Corinthians 5:4,5).

Jesus promised to send the Holy Spirit to the disciples to equip them for carrying the good news into the world. Even after three years of careful teaching by Jesus, even after a dozen appearances by the risen Lord, the disciples lacked understanding and courage. But that would change! "In a few days you will be baptized with the Holy Spirit," Jesus promised at his ascension (Acts 1:5). "You will receive power when the Holy Spirit comes on you; and you will be my witnesses in Jerusalem, and in all Judea and Samaria, and to the ends of the earth" (verse 8). Moreover, the Holy Spirit would make the disciples Jesus' spokesmen with authority to proclaim law and gospel in his name: "[Jesus] breathed on them and said, 'Receive the Holy Spirit. If you forgive anyone his sins, they are forgiven; if you do not forgive them, they are not forgiven'" (John 20:22,23).

His work in the early Christian church

The book of Acts is sometimes called the Holy Spirit's book. It begins with Jesus' promise of a baptism with the Holy Spirit. In the second chapter that promise is kept. The rest of Acts tells how the Holy Spirit directed the believers and blessed their efforts so the good news was preached and the church grew.

In the naval battle of Salamis, the Greek commander Themistocles delayed on shore until nine in the morning. His delay caused great impatience among his men, and some accused him of cowardice and even treason. But the experienced sailor knew that at nine o'clock the land breeze would spring up and fill the sails of the vessels. The wind would drive the ships toward the Persian fleet, and the rowers would be released to be warriors. The strategy worked; the Persian fleet was routed. In a similar way, Jesus' followers must rely on the Holy Spirit (that is, Holy Wind) and not try to accomplish things by their own strength. "Wait for the gift my Father promised, which you have heard me speak about," spoke the Lord Jesus before his ascension (Acts 1:4). The disciples did not have to wait long. Pentecost was only ten days after Jesus ascended.

The events of Pentecost are well known to Christians. Until then, the disciples had been limited in their understanding, frail in their faith, and timid in their testimony. Then as they gathered in one place in Jerusalem, there was a sound like the blowing of a violent wind. When they looked around, they saw tongues of fire that separated and came to rest on each of them. The real wonder is what took place inside each believer. "All of them were filled with the Holy Spirit and began to speak in other tongues as the Spirit enabled them" (Acts 2:4). The most amazing change became evident when Peter stood up and preached to the crowd. Gone was their cowardice; gone was their fuzzy understanding of Jesus' message. Boldly Peter and the others proclaimed the truth: "God has raised this Jesus to life, and we are all witnesses of the fact. Exalted to the right hand of God, he has received from the Father the promised Holy Spirit and has poured out what you now see and hear" (verses 32,33).

The faith, understanding, and courage the apostles displayed at Pentecost continued throughout the book of Acts. When Peter and John were called before the Jewish authorities, "Peter, filled with the Holy Spirit, said to them: '. . . It is by the name of Jesus Christ of Nazareth, whom you crucified but whom God raised from the dead, that this man stands before you healed. Salvation is found in no one else, for there is no other name under heaven given to men by which we must be saved'" (Acts 4:8,10,12). Such powerful witnessing was not limited to a chosen few either. Rather, the Holy Spirit empowered all the believers: "They were all filled with the Holy Spirit and spoke the word of God boldly" (verse 31).

One other change after Pentecost was the scope of the Holy Spirit's work. He began on a large scale to convert Gentiles. We think of Cornelius (Acts 10) and the missionary work of Paul. This is in fulfillment of the prophecy of Joel, who said that in the last days God would pour out his Spirit "on all people" (Joel 2:28; Acts 2:17). This is in contrast to Old Testament times, when the Holy Spirit's saving work was in large part limited to one nation, Israel.

As the early church grew, there was need for different kinds of service. The Holy Spirit saw to it that spiritually qualified workers were found. The Bible describes the first deacons as "men from among you who are known to be full of the Spirit and wisdom" (Acts 6:3). One of the first seven deacons was soon called to even greater service. Stephen, facing martyrdom, got right to the heart of the problem in the enemies of the gospel: "You stiff-necked people . . . you are just like your fathers: You always resist the Holy Spirit!" (7:51). Stephen would pay for this testimony with his life. But the Holy Spirit stood by him even then: "Stephen, full of the Holy Spirit, looked up to

heaven and saw the glory of God, and Jesus standing at
the right hand of God" (verse 55). Stephen died with a
Spirit-given faith and prayer: "Lord Jesus, receive my
spirit" (verse 59).

Ananias and Sapphira gave evidence of an important
truth: you cannot deceive the Holy Spirit. They had
agreed to test the Spirit of the Lord (Acts 5:3), and they
experienced the truth of the law's pronouncement: "Do
not be deceived: God cannot be mocked. A man reaps
what he sows" (Galatians 6:7). Their attempted deception
led to God's judgment—both were struck dead.

On a number of occasions in Acts, the Holy Spirit
demonstrated his presence and approval by special, visible
signs. In Ephesus, for example, there were about 12 men
who had been brought to faith through the preaching of
John the Baptist. Apparently they had received only a
minimal amount of instruction. Perhaps they had heard
John's preaching while visiting in Israel and then had
returned home to Ephesus before they had opportunity to
study in detail. Whatever the reason, they admitted to
Paul, "We have not even heard that there is a Holy Spirit"
(Acts 19:2). Paul, therefore, taught them that John's
preaching was fulfilled in Jesus. The Bible records how the
Holy Spirit showed his approval and backed up the truths
Paul had just shared. "On hearing this, they were baptized
into the name of the Lord Jesus. When Paul placed his
hands on them, the Holy Spirit came on them, and they
spoke in tongues and prophesied" (verses 5,6).

We will look into these special manifestations of the
Spirit more closely when we discuss spiritual gifts in Chapter 8. At this point it is sufficient to say that these spectacular outpourings were not everyday, ordinary gifts experienced by all. Rather, they were quite rare and always were

given for a special purpose. Whether the Holy Spirit's coming on people was marked by miraculous signs or not, the Spirit's work was always to glorify Jesus as the crucified and risen Lord and Savior. We clearly see this in the ministry of Paul, the fierce persecutor of believers who became the greatest Christian missionary.

In Paul's conversion the Holy Spirit worked through hesitant, God-fearing Ananias. Ananias was sent to the blind persecutor Paul (then called Saul) with the words "Brother Saul, the Lord—Jesus who appeared to you on the road as you were coming here—has sent me so that you may see again and be filled with the Holy Spirit" (Acts 9:17). The Bible records the results of Ananias' preaching: "Immediately, something like scales fell from Saul's eyes, and he could see again. He got up and was baptized" (verse 18). In the years that followed Paul's conversion, the Holy Spirit trained him for apostleship.

When it was time for Paul to begin his missionary journeys, the Holy Spirit used the believers in Antioch to set things in motion. "While they were worshiping the Lord and fasting, the Holy Spirit said, 'Set apart for me Barnabas and Saul for the work to which I have called them.' So after they had fasted and prayed, they placed their hands on them and sent them off" (Acts 13:2,3). The Holy Spirit guided and blessed Paul's missionary journeys, leading him relentlessly westward until by the end of Acts the church was established even in faraway Rome, the capital of the empire and the most important city in the world at that time.

Wherever he planted the church, the Holy Spirit supplied evangelists, elders, pastors, teachers, and whatever other workers were needed. While the selection was often made by election of the congregation or by appointment of Paul or another leader, the Holy Spirit was the true source of each call. Paul reminded the Ephesian elders of that fact as he bid them final farewell: "Keep watch over yourselves and all the flock of which the Holy Spirit has made you overseers" (Acts 20:28).

The Holy Spirit continues his work to this day. He preserves and extends the church. He caused the New Testament Scriptures to be written and preserved so we can sit at Jesus' feet and learn from the inspired apostles. Through preaching and through Baptism, the Holy Spirit continues to bring people to faith. He continues to supply to his church needed workers and abilities.

This remains our encouragement and confidence today. The Holy Spirit will not abandon the church in our age either. Even when the odds seem stacked against Christians, even when our efforts seem futile, the Holy Spirit will continue to extend the kingdom of God. The Spirit will make sure the gospel is preached throughout the world and many are called to faith. Even more wonderful, he will use you and me—with our sinful limitations—to be witnesses and build the kingdom.

5

His Main Work

The Holy Spirit's work has one objective—our salvation. In spite of the wondrous love of the Father, in spite of the gracious atonement of the Son, there would be no salvation were it not for the saving work of the Spirit inside us. "If anyone does not have the Spirit of Christ, he does not belong to Christ" (Romans 8:9). The Spirit creates faith in the Savior, Jesus Christ. Through that faith he rescues us from sin and its punishment and makes us the children of God for time and eternity. The formal name for the Holy Spirit's work is sanctification, that is, making saints. In other words, the Spirit calls sinners out of their unbelief and makes them holy people, whose sins are washed away and who are now God's people through

faith in Christ.[10] Sanctification is the main work of the
Holy Spirit. He does that through another work, conversion. In this chapter we will look at what the Bible
teaches about the Spirit's life-giving work of conversion.
But first we will look at how the Spirit prepares people's
hearts for conversion.

Contrition, his "strange" work

Imagine a headline on the front page of this morning's
newspaper reading, "Miracle cure for leprosy found!" How
would you react? Most likely you would skip right over it,
with at most a momentary thought of "That's nice for
those lepers." Since you don't have leprosy and don't
know anyone who does, you would have little interest in
the article and probably would not even read it.

Now imagine that you are one of the 275 patients in
the federal hospital at Carville, Louisiana, the only leprosy
hospital in the continental United States. What would
your reaction be to that headline? You'd read every word
of the article. Then you'd hurry up and down the hallways
of the hospital to share the news. You would want the cure
for yourself! You would want it for your friends!

The Holy Spirit makes us realize that we are such lepers
with a dire need. Our leprosy is called sin. The Spirit-
produced knowledge of our sin is called contrition. The
Spirit makes us aware of our sin and need because he
wants to share the miraculous cure with us.

Jesus said, "When he [the Counselor] comes, he will
convict the world of guilt in regard to sin" (John 16:8).
Isaiah calls convicting the world of sin and bringing sin's
consequences the Lord's "strange work" and his "alien task"
(Isaiah 28:21). The Lutheran Confessions explain: "Therefore the Spirit of Christ must not only comfort but, through

the office of the law, must also convince the world of sin. Thus, even in the New Testament, he must perform what the prophet calls 'a strange deed' (that is, to rebuke) until he comes to his own work (that is, to comfort and to preach about grace)."[11] Before the Holy Spirit can make us glad about our Savior, he must make us sad about our sin.

Before the Holy Spirit begins the task of sanctifying sinners he must bring them to realize their need. To do this, he must trouble the comfortable, that is, make complacent sinners understand the enormity of their sin and the punishment it deserves. "It is not the healthy who need a doctor," Jesus said, "but the sick. . . . I have not come to call the righteous, but sinners" (Matthew 9:12,13). Sick people make use of doctors. People who regard themselves as healthy won't go to a doctor and probably wouldn't follow his advice if they did.

The sinful human will is directed against God. Sinners do not want what God wants. Nor do they want God to be the kind of God he is. This becomes obvious when someone says that a good God would never send anyone to eternal damnation. Thomas Jefferson said that a God who punishes people in hell is a monster. One liberal theologian called God a "dirty bully."[12] Such sentiments illustrate how the natural mind tries to downplay the seriousness of sin. And when it is pointed out that God hates sin and will punish the sinner in hell, the sinful mind concludes God has a problem, not humans.

Contrition is a deep, heartfelt sorrow over sin and a despairing (giving up all hope) of saving oneself. Contrition can be defined as being crushed by our sins or being sorry for our sins. The Augsburg Confession defines contrition as "terrors smiting the conscience with a knowledge of sin."[13]

The Holy Spirit must produce contrition in us. It is not something we can do for ourselves. His tool for working contrition is the law: "Through the law we become conscious of sin" (Romans 3:20). "Indeed I would not have known what sin was except through the law" (7:7). God's law serves as a mirror. Through it the Holy Spirit causes us to see what we really look like to God. In the task of making us aware of our sinfulness, the Holy Spirit has a powerful ally, our consciences.

Contrition is a Spirit-produced change of mind about sin. Our old, sinful self considers sin a source of happiness or profit. Eve, for example, ate the forbidden fruit because she concluded it was "good for food and pleasing to the eye, and also desirable for gaining wisdom" (Genesis 3:6). The Holy Spirit begins by causing sinners to see sin as a source of eternal unhappiness and loss. He teaches sinners to view sin as an offense against God, the almighty Creator who has every right to call his creatures to account on judgment day.

The Spirit leads us to understand that we cannot sidestep God's law or escape God's judgment. The law making its impact on our hearts leads us to despair. We are worthless, doomed, and helpless to do anything about it.

When people have lost all hope of saving themselves, they stand at a fork in the spiritual road: "Godly sorrow brings repentance that leads to salvation and leaves no regret, but worldly sorrow brings death" (2 Corinthians 7:10). If contrite sinners learn nothing more than the law, their worldly sorrow will leave them mired in despair and doomed to death. In fact, terrified sinners hate God all the more because they know there is no way they can measure up to God's standard. They are terrified of God and flee from him as Adam and Eve did in the Garden of

Eden. Contrition is a fruit of the preaching of the law, which by itself cannot save a single sinner. "By observing the law no one will be justified" (Galatians 2:16). On the other hand, if the contrite sinners who then recognize their need for a doctor are brought to the Great Physician, their sorrow can be the gateway to salvation. Contrition, therefore, is "the indispensable preparation for conversion."[14]

A serious error is often spoken with regard to contrition. People say, "God will forgive us if we are sorry for our sins." Notice the devilish "if." For that matter, are we ever sorry enough? Certainly even the most devout Christians find in the recesses of their hearts excuses and rationalizations to justify many of their sins. Certainly even the most God-fearing believers find a twinge of pride that says, "I'm better than many and deserve some favorable consideration by God." God does not forgive us because we are sorry. Contrition is not a meritorious act that earns forgiveness or persuades God to forgive us. Forgiveness comes from God because he is merciful and because of what Jesus has done; it doesn't depend on us achieving a passing score in contrition.

Is the biblical doctrine of contrition outdated in this think-positive, high self-image world? Some would argue that it is bad to preach of sin and destructive of self-image to speak of people's total worthlessness in God's sight. Indeed, if one is only concerned about building people up in their own eyes and only for this world, one could make a convincing argument for that assertion. But remember that God's Word warns of the judgment day to come and an eternity thereafter. People must be brought face to face with their eternal need so the Spirit can lead them to God's gracious solution. Besides, worth is determined by what someone is willing to pay. Believers are precious because Jesus paid out his holy, precious blood for us.

Before we leave the subject of contrition, we should notice that the Christian's need for contrition never ends this side of heaven. In the Small Catechism Martin Luther said that "the old Adam in us should be drowned by daily contrition and repentance, and that all its evil deeds and desires be put to death." Read Romans 7:14-25 for a good example of the frustration Christians feel in their daily battle with sin. That reading also illustrates the feelings of a contrite heart as it approaches God's throne.

Conversion, his saving work

Once the Holy Spirit has troubled the comfortable and complacent sinner with the law, he can get on to what he really wanted to do all along. He can comfort the troubled with the gospel.

"He gave up the ghost," we say. He expired; literally, he breathed out his last breath. Breathing out can signify death. In the reverse of that picture, breathing in brings life—the Holy Wind's breathing in, that is. Jesus put it this way: "The Spirit gives life" (John 6:63). The Holy Spirit entering our hearts causes us to be born again as children of God. This giving of spiritual life to spiritually dead people is called conversion. It happens the instant we are brought to faith in the Savior, Jesus Christ.

Conversion does not take place by stages or degrees, but instantaneously. By nature we are spiritually dead, with no life whatsoever. The first spark of faith in the sinner's heart, therefore, or the first longing after the grace of God in Christ, constitutes conversion. Simply put, either a person has faith or doesn't; there is no in-between stage.

In conversion the Holy Spirit takes a blind, dead enemy of God and calls him by the gospel. The gospel is the good news that Jesus Christ has done everything necessary for the salvation of sinners. The gospel announces that Jesus, as true God and true man, kept the law of God perfectly in our place. Jesus suffered the punishment we deserve for our sins when he died innocently on the cross. Then Jesus arose from the dead to give us and all sinners the assurance that we are forgiven. We are declared innocent. God no longer needs to punish us.

To bring this gospel to us, the Holy Spirit uses the Word of God and the sacraments of Baptism and the Lord's Supper. These are the means of grace, or the tools the Holy Spirit uses. We should not expect the Holy Spirit to fall upon us out of the clear blue. We can expect him to come to us only through these means.

The Holy Spirit plants saving faith in our hearts through the means of grace. He guides us to believe the message that we have the forgiveness of sins through Jesus. This is why the Apostles' Creed speaks of the forgiveness of sins in the Third Article in connection with the Holy Spirit. Certainly Jesus has acquired the forgiveness of sins as our Savior. One could therefore speak of the forgiveness of sins in the Second Article of the Apostles' Creed. However, if we are not brought to faith by the Holy Spirit, we will not personally receive the blessing of forgiveness. When the Holy Spirit brings us to faith, he makes forgiveness our own personal possession.

Saving faith involves several components. First there is knowledge. People cannot believe what they do not know. Hence, faith without knowledge is an impossibility. The second component is assent or acceptance as truth. People cannot believe in something they regard as false and unreliable. The third component is trust. People must place their confidence in those facts they regard as true and rely on them to help.

In 1859 Charles Blondin made a name for himself by walking across Niagara Falls on an 1,100-foot tightrope suspended 160 feet above the falls. To climb on his back and let him carry you across the falls would require faith. It would not be sufficient to know that Blondin had walked across before. It also wouldn't be enough to accept intellectually that he could do it again. To benefit from Blondin's services, you would have to entrust your life into his hands and let him carry you across. In a similar way the Holy Spirit leads our hearts to trust in Jesus alone for salvation. That is the Spirit's main work.

Placing one's faith in the right object is the important thing. I can believe with all my heart that Kleenex will cure the common cold, and I can use it by the boxful. That won't cure my cold, however, because Kleenex has no curative powers. I can believe in Kleenex all I want, but that faith will not help me. In fact, faith in the wrong object can hurt me. I can get up in the middle of the night with a headache and swallow some small white tablets that I firmly believe to be aspirins. If by mistake I took roach poison, however, I could end up dead. In that case, you could inscribe on my tombstone, "He died in faith." Even in secular things what matters is not faith, but on what we place our faith. Saving faith rests on Jesus Christ and relies on him for rescue.

Only the Holy Spirit can work saving faith. The Bible tells us that. "I tell you that . . . no one can say, 'Jesus is Lord,' except by the Holy Spirit" (1 Corinthians 12:3). This truth is captured by Martin Luther in his explanation to the Third Article of the Apostles' Creed: "I believe that

I cannot by my own thinking or choosing believe in Jesus Christ, my Lord, or come to him. But the Holy Spirit has called me by the gospel, enlightened me with his gifts, sanctified and kept me in the true faith."

Contrition, as we said before, is a change of mind regarding sin. Faith, and therefore conversion, is a change of mind regarding salvation. We can diagram it this way:

God wants man to be saved by grace. ———→
←——— Unconverted man wants to be saved by works.
Converted man wants to be saved by grace. ———→

A person who thought he could get to heaven by being good realizes that he can be saved only by what Christ has done for him. The cross of Christ, which had seemed foolishness, now makes the most wonderful sense.

Words used for conversion

The picture in the word *conversion* is that of a person being turned around in his tracks. He was relying on himself and going straight down the road to hell until he was converted. Then he was turned around, 180 degrees, in his thoughts and direction. Relying on Jesus alone, he is headed up the path to heaven.

The Bible uses other picture words for conversion:

- *Rebirth, regeneration, or being born again*—"No one can see the kingdom of God unless he is born again" (John 3:3). We were born the first time as sinful children of sinful parents. We need to be born a second time as children of God.

- *Quickening or resurrection*—"Because of his great love for us, God, who is rich in mercy, made us alive with Christ even when we were dead in transgressions" (Ephesians 2:4,5). Coming to faith is a rising from spiritual death to spiritual life.

- *Illumination, enlightenment, or turning on the light*—
  God "called you out of darkness into his wonderful
  light" (1 Peter 2:9). We were groping around in the
  darkness, blind and unable to see the way to God,
  until the Holy Spirit entered our hearts and turned
  on the light so we could see the way to heaven.

Conversion, regeneration, quickening, enlightenment and the
other terms listed in this paragraph are synonymous. They
should not be viewed as successive stages or steps on the
way to becoming a full-fledged child of God. They denote
the moment the Spirit brings an unbeliever to faith.

The word *repentance* is closely related to *conversion*. The
Bible uses *repentance* in two ways. In its narrower sense
repentance refers to sorrow over sin and desisting from sin.
In this usage it is closely akin in meaning to *contrition*. In
Luke 24:47, for example, Jesus distinguishes between the
preaching of repentance and the preaching of remission of
sins: "Repentance and forgiveness of sins will be preached
in his name to all nations." In its broader sense *repentance*
includes turning to Jesus in faith for his forgiveness, as
illustrated by the verse "Unless you repent, you too will all
perish" (Luke 13:5). In the case of someone who previously was an unbeliever, this repentance is conversion.
The changed life and good works that follow conversion
are known as "the fruits of repentance." Repentance is not
limited to first-time believers, however. Christians
throughout their entire lives must sorrow daily over their
sins, trust in Jesus' forgiveness, and seek to amend their
sinful lives.

Conversion, the Spirit's work alone

Conversion is the work of the Holy Spirit alone; it is
not a cooperative or team effort involving the human will.

The Formula of Concord states that truth: "For the conversion of our corrupted will, which is nothing else but a resurrection of the will from spiritual death, is solely and alone the work of God, just as the bodily resurrection of the flesh is to be ascribed to God alone."[15] Conversion, or the creating of faith, is an act of divine grace.

> God . . . made his light shine in our hearts to give us the light of the knowledge of the glory of God in the face of Christ. (2 Corinthians 4:6)

> It is by grace you have been saved, through faith—and this not from yourselves, it is the gift of God—not by works, so that no one can boast. (Ephesians 2:8,9)

False teachers and misguided Christians have tried to give humans some credit for conversion. Some have taught that humans are the cause of their salvation, saying that they can keep the commandments of God with the proper use of their own spiritual powers.[16] Others have taught that humans have imperfect spiritual powers but that with the help of God, humans can keep the commandments and attain salvation.[17] Still others say there remains a spark of spiritual power in people, so that they can accept the forgiving grace of God when it is given to them.[18]

In opposition to all these false teachings, the Bible clearly teaches that God converts the sinner while the sinner is purely passive. In conversion, humans are like blocks or stones. In fact, they are worse than blocks or stones; they are enemies of God by nature. Therefore, they actively resist the operation of the Spirit until they are converted. Consider the Formula of Concord once again: "Man of himself or by his natural powers is unable to do anything and cannot assist in any way toward his conversion."[19] For people to claim responsibility in any way for their conversion denies Christianity's central doctrine that we are saved by grace alone.

We see some of the same errors in the modern-day church. Those who speak of "making a decision for Christ" and who stress the importance of a "conversion experience" commonly place the emphasis on what the sinner does rather than the Spirit. We can see the same danger also in the expression "All you have to do is accept Christ."

Recognizing that faith is entirely the working of the Holy Spirit will clear up questions some have about baptizing infants. When we realize that divine intervention is necessary for anyone to come to faith, then certainly almighty God can work also in the very young. He can keep his promise: "Baptism . . . now saves you also" (1 Peter 3:21). "He saved us through the washing of rebirth and renewal by the Holy Spirit" (Titus 3:5).

Why are some saved and not others? This is one of the most difficult questions Christians will ponder and one we are not able to answer to the satisfaction of our human reason. Scripture affirms that God is the sole cause of a person's conversion and salvation. On the other hand, it clearly teaches that the unbeliever is the sole cause of his damnation.

Jesus taught this truth when he lamented over Jerusalem: "How often I have longed to gather your children together, as a hen gathers her chicks under her wings, but you were not willing" (Matthew 23:37). Stephen made the same point to the unbelieving Jewish leaders: "You stiff-necked people, with uncircumcised hearts and ears! You are just like your fathers: You always resist the Holy Spirit!" (Acts 7:51).

Sinners can reject the Spirit's working; the Spirit does not force himself upon us. Therefore, although we cannot save ourselves, we can condemn ourselves. An illustration may help us understand this truth. People can destroy their lives by suicide, but they are unable to restore the lives they have destroyed.

The Bible does not explain why, concerning two similar sinners (like David and Saul or Peter and Judas), one is saved and another is not, and we dare not go beyond what God has told us. The Formula of Concord describes the God-pleasing attitude to have in this regard: "Because God has reserved this mystery to his own wisdom and not revealed anything concerning it in the Word, still less has commanded us to explore it through our speculations . . . , therefore we are not, on the basis of our speculations, to make our own deductions, draw conclusions, or brood over it, but cling solely to his revealed Word, to which he directs us."[20]

So it rests: God desires the salvation of all and calls to faith; some reject Jesus' rescue and are lost because of their unbelief. The message is clear: To God alone be the glory! Thank and praise him for the faith he has given you!

6

Good Works from a New Nature

The Holy Spirit does not stop his work once he has called us to life through conversion. Rather, he continues to work in us to produce the fruits of faith. Just as a candle sends forth light from the moment it begins to burn until it is extinguished, so Christian living begins the very moment faith is kindled in the heart, and it continues as long as the light of faith burns. True faith in the heart will have an effect on the life of a person, for faith always shows.

In the previous chapter we saw that the term *sanctification* can describe the full scope of the Holy Spirit's work of making saints, beginning with the call to faith. *Sanctification* is also used in a narrower sense. In this usage it refers to the Holy Spirit's work in the heart and life of a person who is already a Christian. It refers to the Spirit's efforts to lead the Christian to a life of good works. Service to God and obedience to his commandments are the inevitable results of conversion. Luther speaks beautifully of the power in us through faith:

> Oh, faith is a living, busy, active, mighty thing, so that it is impossible for it not to be constantly doing what is good. Likewise, faith does not ask if good works are to be done, but before one can ask, faith has already done them and is constantly active.[21]

Saints = new creatures

Saint is the Bible's name for a believer in Jesus Christ. Saint means "a sanctified person, one who has been made holy and is set aside for sacred service."

> Jesus also suffered outside the city gate to make the people holy through his own blood. (Hebrews 13:12)

> Therefore, if anyone is in Christ, he is a new creation; the old has gone, the new has come! (2 Corinthians 5:17)

The Holy Spirit works in saints with the goal of leading each one to live an increasingly godly life. Step by step the Spirit renews each saint into Christ's image.

> You were taught, with regard to your former way of life, to put off your old self, which is being corrupted by its deceitful desires; to be made new in the attitude of your minds; and to put on the new self, created to be like God in true righteousness and holiness. (Ephesians 4:22-24)

The new nature we have through faith makes itself known through a life of good works. Humans cannot decide which works are pleasing to God. Only God can do that. In his Word God says that two things are necessary for a work to qualify as good in his eyes.

First of all, a good work must conform to God's law. The godly person is described as one whose "delight is in the law of the LORD, and on his law he meditates day and night" (Psalm 1:2). The Formula of Concord emphasizes the need for the teaching of God's law: "Believers, furthermore, require the teaching of the law so that they will not be thrown back on their own holiness and piety and under the pretext of the Holy Spirit's guidance set up a self-elected service of God without his Word and command."[22]

The second identifying mark of a good work is that it proceeds from the proper motive. "Without faith it is impossible to please God" (Hebrews 11:6). Two persons may do exactly the same work outwardly. If one does it out of fear of punishment or in the hope of reward and the other does it out of love for God and in gratitude for God's mercies, only the second instance is a good work in God's eyes. A good work is a happy "thank you" to God. Therefore, only a Christian can do a truly good work.

Each of us has a self-righteous Pharisee inside who feels that good works are our achievements and should win merit in God's sight. Such a payment-for-services-rendered approach, however, displays self-righteous pride and total ignorance of the fact that we cannot achieve perfection, God's minimum standard. The power to do a truly good work—one that springs from the proper motivation and is in keeping with God's revealed will—cannot come from within our sinful selves. The power must come from the Holy Spirit, who dwells in the heart and makes it his temple. The Bible tells us simply, "It is God who works in you to will and to act according to his good purpose" (Philippians 2:13).

In contrast to the unbeliever's natural hatred of what God wants, the saint consents to God's will and even finds joy in it: "In my inner being I delight in God's law" (Romans 7:22). Even more amazing, the new creature we become through faith lives according to God's will:

> We died to sin; how can we live in it any longer? We were therefore buried with him through baptism into death in order that, just as Christ was raised from the dead through the glory of the Father, we too may live a new life. For we know that our old self was crucified with him so that the body of sin might be done away with, that we should no longer be slaves to sin. In the same way, count yourselves dead to sin but alive to God in Christ Jesus. (Romans 6:2,4,6,11)

When we confess our sins in church each Sunday, we are dumping a garbage bag full of sins and shortcomings on the altar. Jesus takes care of our moral trash for us, washing away our sins and drowning them in the depths of the sea. Jesus does more than get rid of our filthy garbage, however. He was righteous for us, and he credits his righteousness to us. We walk out of church as righteous children of God! Our purpose in life is not just to fill our garbage bag again so we have something to dump on the altar next Sunday. We go out dressed in Christ—not to find the nearest mud puddle and get filthy again, but to glorify and serve God. On Confirmation Sunday we customarily dress our young people in white robes—to show them who they are. The white robe says, "You are a righteous child of God!" All believers in Jesus Christ are God's children, washed clean and empowered by God to serve him.

We serve God by being faithful to him in whatever station in life he has assigned to us. A husband serves God by being a loving, self-sacrificing head to his family. A mother glorifies God by preparing meals, washing clothes, and kissing away hurts for the children God has entrusted to her. A child serves God by respecting and obeying the parents God has given—as well as by making his bed and clearing the table after meals. The property owner serves God when, out of gratitude for what God has given him, he takes care of his property—when he mows the lawn, washes his car, and paints the shutters. The employee serves God by giving an honest day's work, even if the rest of the crew is shirking duty. The church member shows she is God's new creation by regular Sunday attendance and by volunteering where needed. The citizen glorifies God by obeying the law, paying taxes, doing good to others, picking up litter, and voting for the best candidate.

We are the children of God, dressed in the robes of Christ's righteousness. The Holy Spirit gives many opportunities for us to let our light shine before others so that they may see our good deeds and praise our Father in heaven (Matthew 5:16).

Struggling with the old sinful nature

This all sounds great, but we know there's a problem. The apostle Paul describes our situation this way: "I have the desire to do what is good, but I cannot carry it out. For what I do is not the good I want to do; no, the evil I do not want to do—this I keep on doing" (Romans 7:18,19). Every saint remains a sinner and faces a lifelong struggle. There is a war raging inside us. "For the sinful nature desires what is contrary to the Spirit, and the Spirit what is contrary to the sinful nature. They are in conflict with each other, so that you do not do what you want" (Galatians 5:17).

Our old sinful nature (also known as the old man, the old Adam, and the old self) remains thoroughly corrupt. It has joined with Satan and the sinful world to fight Christ to the end and is a committed member of the evil alliance. We are not talking about limited warfare, about a fight in which no one gets hurt or a gentlemen's agreement binds all to rules of fairness. Sanctification does not reform our old sinful nature or make it more mellow and open to godliness. That is not possible. Our old nature will kick and claw and bite to the bitter end of our earthly lives.

Our old sinful nature cannot be converted, but it can be crucified. We dare not compromise with it, for eternity is at stake.

> If you live according to the sinful nature, you will die; but if by the Spirit you put to death the misdeeds of the body, you will live. (Romans 8:13)

> Those who belong to Christ Jesus have crucified the sinful nature with its passions and desires. (Galatians 5:24)

We need only recall Jesus' graphic words to see the seriousness of the battle:

> If your hand or your foot causes you to sin, cut it off and throw it away. It is better for you to enter life maimed or crippled than to have two hands or two feet and be thrown into eternal fire. And if your eye causes you to sin, gouge it out and throw it away. It is better for you to enter life with one eye than to have two eyes and be thrown into the fire of hell. (Matthew 18:8,9)

We have a strong helper in the struggle against sin, Satan, and our old sinful nature. The Bible assures us that the Paraclete, the Comforter, who stands at our side, battles along with us: "I will put my Spirit in you and move you to follow my decrees and be careful to keep my laws" (Ezekiel 36:27).

While sinners can do nothing to produce faith in their hearts, saints can cooperate in resisting Satan and bearing the fruits of faith. Believers can cooperate, that is, because the Holy Spirit is working in them and empowering them. Driven along by the Holy Wind, for example, we can make regular and faithful use of God's Word. "Like new-born babies, crave pure spiritual milk, so that by it you may grow up in your salvation" (1 Peter 2:2).

Although the law cannot give strength for Christian living, it is a valuable guide for the godly life. The gospel, on the other hand, creates love for God in our hearts by reminding us of God's great love for us. In turn, the gospel stimulates us to follow Jesus' example and love one another. Through the Scriptures we receive comfort as we see that even the greatest saints were obliged continually to wage war against their evil flesh. Moreover, the Bible enables us, like Jesus, to meet Satan's tempting with appropriate passages of Scripture. When confronted with Satan's temptations, Jesus did not seek guidance in a special revelation. Instead, he relied on the written Word of God (Luke 4:1-13).

The Lutheran Confessions state, "Our best works, even after the grace of the Gospel has been received, are still weak and not at all pure."[23] We need look no further than Sunday morning to see proof of this statement. Very likely prior to our departure for church, especially if it's a cold winter's day or a scorching hot summer day, thoughts enter our minds that are something short of cheerfulness and enthusiasm at the privilege of worshiping our gracious God. Probably a few words are spoken to family members abruptly or harshly about hurrying up or we'll be late.

Once in the service, our mind wanders during the prayers, we fight slumber during the sermon, and we have less than loving thoughts for the screaming child, the visitor with a ring in his or her nose, or the stewardship board's appeal for increased offerings. Then we cross paths with that member whom we have difficulty loving as a brother or sister. We sin, you see, even in a good deed like going to church. Luther pointed to that reality when he said:

> This life, therefore, is not godliness but the process of becoming godly, not health but getting well, not being but becoming, not rest but exercise. We are not now what we shall be, but we are on the way. The process is not yet finished, but it is actively going on. This is not the goal but it is the right road. At present, everything does not gleam and sparkle, but everything is being cleansed.[24]

The following ditty puts it in more everyday terms:

> I ain't what I should be;
> I ain't what I'm going to be;
> But, thank God, I ain't what I was!

Saints will be at different levels of sanctification. The weak faith succumbs to temptation more easily than the strong faith. It produces fewer good works and gives way to fear and doubt in face of danger. If one seems to be living a more godly life, thank God for it—that godliness happens only by the power of the Holy Spirit in that person. If other Christians seem to be lacking in godliness, pray for them and encourage them. The goal of each saint is continually to increase and grow. We are urged to do "works of service, so that the body of Christ may be built up until we all reach unity in the faith and in the knowledge of the

Son of God and become mature, attaining to the whole measure of the fullness of Christ" (Ephesians 4:12,13).

By the grace of God, we can make progress in the daily struggle to drown the old sinful nature and let the new Christian nature live in us. "Offer yourselves to God, as those who have been brought from death to life; and offer the parts of your body to him as instruments of righteousness" (Romans 6:13).

Good works are necessary

The fact that sanctification is incomplete must not be abused by the Christian as an excuse to make no effort at growth. On the contrary, it should move the believer constantly to strive after holiness in the fear of God. This is God's will for us, his children.

> Make every effort . . . to be holy; without holiness no one will see the Lord. (Hebrews 12:14)

> It is God's will that you should be sanctified: that you should avoid sexual immorality; that each of you should learn to control his own body in a way that is holy and honorable. For God did not call us to be impure, but to live a holy life. (1 Thessalonians 4:3,4,7)

The God-pleasing conclusion for us to draw is obvious: "Just as he who called you is holy, so be holy in all you do; for it is written: 'Be holy, because I am holy'" (1 Peter 1:15,16).

Good works are necessary. The Bible says:

> What good is it, my brothers, if a man claims to have faith but has no deeds? Can such faith save him? Suppose a brother or sister is without clothes and daily food. If one of you says to him, "Go, I wish you well; keep warm and well fed," but does nothing about his physical needs, what good

> is it? In the same way, faith by itself, if it is not accompa-
> nied by action, is dead. As the body without the spirit is
> dead, so faith without deeds is dead. (James 2:14-17,26)

We dare not minimize the importance of good works in our lives. They are the necessary, absolutely essential evidence of faith in our hearts. Moreover, Jesus' parable of the final judgment makes it clear that the judge will point to our works to show whether we were believers or not. Read Matthew 25:31-46.

Conversion, with its gift of faith, comes first. That is what saves. Fruits of faith follow as the inevitable consequences and proofs of faith. We must never reverse the order. It is wrong to teach, as some churches do, that our good works lead to salvation. This false teaching suggests that God sees those who are trying to be godly and then, because of their sincere efforts, steps in to forgive and justify them. The cause of salvation in such a false scenario is goodness in the person rather than the grace of God. By contrast, as we have seen, Scripture teaches that believers do not do good works in order to be saved, but because they have been saved.

The reward of good works

God in his grace has even more goodness in store for us. The Holy Spirit calls us to faith and produces the fruits of faith in us—all by his doing. Then God blesses us—rewards us!—as if those good works were something special we had achieved.

In many places the Bible emphatically assures believers that their good works will be liberally rewarded. To those who face persecution for the gospel's sake, Jesus promises, "Rejoice in that day and leap for joy, because great is your reward in heaven" (Luke 6:23). To those who love their enemies and do good to them, Jesus promises, "Your reward will be great, and you will be sons of the Most High, because he is kind to the ungrateful and wicked" (verse 35). To those who plant and to those who water in the church, Paul promises, "Each will be rewarded according to his own labor" (1 Corinthians 3:8). The writer to the Hebrews assures us, "God . . . will not forget your work and the love you have shown him as you have helped his people and continue to help them" (6:10). In fact, speaking of the believers entering heaven, Jesus says, "Their deeds will follow them" (Revelation 14:13). Rewards for good works are granted both in this world and in the hereafter: "Godliness has value for all things, holding promise for both the present life and the life to come" (1 Timothy 4:8). God has not revealed to us what the reward will be in each instance. He may bring special blessings in our lives now. He may grant a greater degree of glory in heaven.

When speaking of God rewarding our good works, however, the Lutheran Confessions properly explain, "In the proclamation of rewards grace is displayed."[25] The reward for good works comes not because of the believer's merit, but because of God's grace. On the other hand, all who demand a reward not only forfeit God's reward of grace, but also risk their salvation. Read Matthew 19:27–20:16 and notice how Jesus teaches both of the truths just stated. There are rewards: The disciples are promised 12 thrones in heaven and "everyone who has left houses or brothers or sisters or father or mother or children or fields for my sake will receive a hundred times as much" (19:29). Then immediately after that promise, almost as if to show that Jesus knew it could be misunderstood, he tells the parable of the workers in the vineyard to teach that rewards come purely from the goodness of the Lord, who graciously gives out what is his to give. Jesus twice explains: "The last [those who deserve nothing good from him] will be first [because of his grace], and the first [the self-righteous who outwardly serve God] will be last [and out of the kingdom altogether]" (20:16; see also 19:30).

A life lived or a work done to earn reward ceases to be a fruit of faith and love. On the other hand, through his promises of gracious blessings, God encourages Christians zealously to perform good works. Martin Luther said that through the Bible passages that speak of reward "the godly are awakened, comforted, and raised up to go forward, persevere, and conquer in doing good and enduring evil, lest they should grow weary or lose heart."[26]

Although our works are imperfect and impure because of sin, they nevertheless are acceptable and pleasing to God. We do not learn this from the message of God's law. The law continues to hold before our eyes the fact that "all our righteous acts are like filthy rags" (Isaiah 64:6). Rather, the gospel teaches that our spiritual sacrifices are acceptable to God through Jesus Christ (1 Peter 2:5). Jesus washes away our imperfections and then blesses us for our efforts. The message again is clear: To God alone be the glory!

7

Gifts for All Believers

Our imaginations easily run wild when we try to imagine what life is like in heaven, God's perfect dwelling place, his holy temple. The Bible, especially in the visions given to Saint John, recorded in Revelation, describes heaven as a place of perfect peace and tranquillity, of awesome grandeur and glory, devoid of all malice and evil.

Now let your imagination run for a while on the thought that already now a believer is such a wondrous dwelling place of God. "Don't you know that you yourselves are God's temple and that God's Spirit lives in you? . . . God's temple is sacred, and you are that temple" (1 Corinthians 3:16,17). Inside each Christian is a place of faith, peace, and tranquillity, a thing of beauty, a temple where no malice or evil is found. At least that is the kind of divine temple the Holy Spirit wants to make within us! Through the gospel in the Word and sacraments, the Holy Spirit pours into us the gifts that make us a dwelling fit for the King.

Faith, his prime gift

"Repent and be baptized, every one of you, in the name of Jesus Christ for the forgiveness of your sins. And you will receive the gift of the Holy Spirit. The promise is for you and your children and for all who are far off—for all whom the Lord our God will call" (Acts 2:38,39). With these words Peter called the crowd to faith on the first Pentecost. Notice well the means that were used: the gospel message was preached and Baptism with water was administered. Through these means the Holy Spirit was given to the people as a gift so he could dwell in their hearts and bring his gifts into their lives.

We have seen earlier that the Holy Spirit's prime work is to glorify Jesus (John 16:14,15) by testifying about Jesus and what he has done (15:26). It follows logically, then, that the Spirit's first and foremost gift is saving faith. The Holy Spirit causes the testimony of Jesus to take root in our hearts and grow into faith. In this way the Spirit brings glory to Jesus by building up Jesus' body, the church.

We all need a spiritual tutor: "The man without the Spirit does not accept the things that come from the Spirit of God, for they are foolishness to him, and he cannot understand them, because they are spiritually discerned" (1 Corinthians 2:14). The *New Evangelical Translation: New Testament* (the predecessor to the *God's Word* translation) captures that last phrase clearly: "because one must have the Spirit to judge them correctly." Spiritual discernment, the ability to judge wisely and correctly in religious matters, therefore, comes solely through the Holy Spirit. "I tell you that no one who is speaking by the Spirit of God says, 'Jesus be cursed,' and no one can say, 'Jesus is Lord,' except by the Holy Spirit" (12:3). Spiritual discernment to recognize Jesus as Lord is, in a word, faith. The Holy Spirit gives such saving faith freely to each Christian.

Companion gifts of faith

With the gift of faith come many other spiritual gifts as well.

"May the God of hope fill you . . . so that you may overflow with hope by the power of the Holy Spirit," Paul prays for the Romans and in turn for us (Romans 15:13). Hope is an added benefit of faith, as the Bible tells us: "Faith is being sure of what we hope for and certain of what we do not see" (Hebrews 11:1). Christian hope can be defined as a confident longing for the things God has promised. When our hope is based on the promises of our faithful God, there is nothing uncertain about it. God keeps his promises! Our hope is a fact; it just hasn't happened yet. In the midst of life with its frequent troubles and heartaches, we have a sure and certain hope. We have the hope of a better world to follow in heaven, and we have the hope of a God who will stand by our side to bring us safely there.

This hope, this certainty, is a gift of the Holy Spirit. "We rejoice in the hope of the glory of God. Not only so but we also rejoice in our sufferings, because we know that suffering produces perseverance; perseverance, character; and character, hope. And hope does not disappoint us, because God has poured out his love into our hearts by the Holy Spirit, whom he has given us" (Romans 5:2-5).

"All you need is love," the golden oldies radio station plays again and again. Another of its favorites says, "What the world needs now is love, sweet love. It's the only thing that there's just too little of." The Christian knows that such lyrics are missing the point. The love we need is there—free and full—for "God so loved the world . . ." (John 3:16). As a gift of the Holy Spirit, the believer knows the amazing love of God encompasses us. "Greater love has no one than this, that he lay down his life for his friends" (15:13). But Jesus loved us even more than that because he laid down his life for us when we were still his bitterest enemies. "This is how God showed his love among us: He sent his one and only Son into the world that we might live through him. This is love: not that we loved God, but that he loved us and sent his Son as an atoning sacrifice for our sins" (1 John 4:9,10).

The Spirit also comforts and encourages us through the assurance that we have received the Spirit of sonship (Romans 8:15). "God sent the Spirit of his Son into our hearts, the Spirit who calls out, '*Abba*, Father.' So you are no longer a slave, but a son; and since you are a son, God has made you also an heir" (Galatians 4:6,7). No longer do we tremble before the awesome majesty of the almighty Creator and perfect Judge of the universe; no longer do we try to hide from his all-seeing eyes. Rather, the Holy Spirit has taught us to know him as our "dear Father" (*Abba*) in heaven.

You may recall a famous picture from President Kennedy's years. The president sat at his imposing desk in the Oval Office in the midst of the Cuban Missile Crisis—at a time when our nation stood on the brink of nuclear world war. On the carpet underneath that desk the President's young son was playing peacefully, happily with his toys. In just this way, while the world stumbles in chaos toward judgment day, we can live our lives in peace, oblivious to all that swirls around us. We are God's dear children. Our heavenly Father has things under his control, and he is keeping his eye on us!

Part of the spiritual discernment the Holy Spirit gives with faith is the ability to judge all things. The Spirit causes us to know *the* truth, namely, God's eternal truth. "When he, the Spirit of truth, comes, he will guide you into all truth," Jesus promised (John 16:13). Firmly grounded in God's truth, found in the Bible, Christians have the basis to make judgments on the spiritual matters that come before them. Believers can evaluate what they see and hear on the basis of the revealed truth of God, confident that the Holy Spirit will assist them in applying that truth correctly. On the other hand, the worldly wise, no matter how much human education they have received, are not able to make valid judgments regarding Christians or the truth they confess. Paul put it this way: "The spiritual man makes judgments about all things, but he himself is not subject to any man's judgment: 'For who has known the mind of the Lord that he may instruct him?' But we have the mind of Christ" (1 Corinthians 2:15,16). The simplest Christian armed with the Scriptures and guided by the Holy Spirit is wiser in the matters of God than the most highly educated unbeliever. In fact, before entering school for the first time, most believers have learned the most profound truth of all: "Jesus loves me this I know, for the Bible tells me so."

Fruits of the Spirit

The Holy Spirit gives us faith, hope, love, sonship, and truth. These gifts flow from God and are given for us to

enjoy and use. The Spirit dwelling inside us also trans-
forms our characters. He works in us to produce reflections
of the divine in our daily dealings. Those divine characteristics he produces are called the fruits of the Spirit, or the
fruits of faith. They are produced in all believers and are
traits each Christian should strive to display abundantly in
this life.

"The fruit of the Spirit is love, joy, peace, patience,
kindness, goodness, faithfulness, gentleness and self-
control. . . . Since we live by the Spirit, let us keep in step
with the Spirit" (Galatians 5:22,23,25). The love spoken
of in these verses is not the same as the love we discussed
earlier in this chapter. There the love was God's love that
we receive and enjoy. This Galatians verse speaks about
the love that God produces in us. It's the love the Bible
speaks of when it says, "We love because he [God] first
loved us" (1 John 4:19). Motivated by God's love for us,
we now become lovers. Out of selfish, self-centered people
the Holy Spirit makes saints who truly reflect Christ-like
love to those around them. This is a miraculous change
from our natural attitude toward others, especially our
enemies. It is a change in character worked by the power
of the Holy Spirit within us.

In the midst of the troubles and heartaches of this life,
the Christian has joy. That too is a miracle. Our minds
look at the headlines in the daily newspapers and at the
problems in our lives. We look at the friends who disappoint us and the relatives who let us down. Our minds
often see nothing to be joyful about. But then our faith
kicks in. It sees the love of God, the hope of heaven, and
the certainty that our heavenly Father rules all things for
our good. The Holy Spirit empowers our faith to say to our
minds: "I don't care what you say, Mind. God rules, and

I will joyfully trust in him!" Earthly joys are—at best—temporary and doomed eventually to disappoint; the Spirit's joy is eternal and will never fail us.

The Spirit produces peace. The Christian, at peace in his conscience, at peace with his God, at peace regarding what the future holds, enjoys personal peacefulness. Moreover, the Holy Spirit converts that inner peace into action so that the Christian becomes the living embodiment of Jesus' words "Blessed are the peacemakers" (Matthew 5:9).

Patience, kindness, goodness, faithfulness, gentleness, and self-control are characteristics in short supply in a dog-eat-dog world. On the other hand, all were in bountiful supply in the life of Jesus Christ. In this he set an example for us. Now the Holy Spirit produces these characteristics in all of Jesus' followers. There is something unnatural in such characteristics. In fact, the natural mind sees them as dangerous because "people will take advantage of you and walk all over you." The natural mind may often be right in that regard. The Holy Spirit makes us unnatural, however; he makes us godly. The Spirit makes us truly want to follow Jesus' example and to do what pleases God. As for those who take advantage of us or misuse our godliness, we will let the Lord handle that.

Consider a few additional examples of the miraculous changes in character the Spirit produces. His working is even more awesome when you consider the weak, sinful material he has to work with.

> The wisdom that comes from heaven is first of all pure; then peace-loving, considerate, submissive, full of mercy and good fruit, impartial and sincere. (James 3:17)

> Therefore, as God's chosen people, holy and dearly loved, clothe yourselves with compassion, kindness, humility,

gentleness and patience. Bear with each other and forgive whatever grievances you may have against one another. Forgive as the Lord forgave you. And over all these virtues put on love, which binds them all together in perfect unity. Let the peace of Christ rule in your hearts. . . . And whatever you do, whether in word or deed, do it all in the name of the Lord Jesus, giving thanks to God the Father through him. (Colossians 3:12-15,17)

Another important fruit is the courage to witness for Christ and, through our witness, to call others to faith. At his ascension Jesus promised his disciples, "You will receive power when the Holy Spirit comes on you; and you will be my witnesses in Jerusalem, and in all Judea and Samaria, and to the ends of the earth" (Acts 1:8). While this promise was fulfilled in a spectacular way on Pentecost, it is not limited to the original 12 disciples. That is first shown us by the parting words of Jesus we just read. Those 12 men would not by themselves be able to witness "to the ends of the earth." The completion of such worldwide witnessing would require many witnesses over many years.

The wider intent of Jesus' promise is demonstrated also in the events that followed the first Pentecost. "A great persecution broke out against the church at Jerusalem, and all except the apostles were scattered throughout Judea and Samaria. Those who had been scattered preached the word wherever they went" (Acts 8:1,4). Jesus gave this command to his church: "Go and make disciples of all nations. . . . And surely I am with you always, to the very end of the age" (Matthew 28:19,20). This Great Commission implies that the Holy Spirit will continue to make and equip witnesses in every era of time to the very end.

Use of the Spirit's gifts

Just as an apple tree produces apples, so those who are temples of the Spirit produce the fruits of the Spirit. Every apple tree does not produce fruit equal in quantity or quality, however. In the same way Christians enjoy and reflect the Spirit's gifts in varying degrees. Our goal is to cultivate the gifts and fruits of the Spirit, faithfully using the Word, Baptism, and the Lord's Supper to grow spiritually.

To help us reach our goal, we have an ever-present helper. We are reminded of his presence each time we hear the apostolic blessing in a worship service: "The fellowship of the Holy Spirit be with you all" (2 Corinthians 13:14). The Spirit comes to us to bring peace and purity. He descends with a sword, "which is the word of God" (Ephesians 6:17). He uses that Word to battle the sin and weakness that hinder our enjoyment of his gifts.

8

Foundational and Confirmatory Gifts

The Greek word *charisma* (plural: *charismata*) means "a gift of grace," a gift of God's undeserved love. It is the Bible's word for the special gifts the Holy Spirit freely gives to God's people. Some of the Spirit's *charismata*, such as instantaneous healing or speaking in tongues, are spectacular. Others, like teaching or showing mercy, may seem ordinary and unexciting. All the Spirit's gifts, however, are intended for the good of the church.

The modern-day charismatic movement has adopted the term *charisma* as its own and seeks to reclaim the supernatural gifts of the Spirit and use them in the church today. Charismatics have a fascination especially with the spectacular gifts of speaking in tongues, healing, and prophecy.

Fascination with the supernatural gifts of the Spirit has centered historically in the Pentecostal family of churches. As their name implies, these churches attempt on a regular basis to relive the miraculous outpouring of the Spirit on the first Pentecost. In the past, Pentecostal churches were relegated to the fringes of Christianity. Lately, however, the charismatic movement has made inroads into most denominations in the United States. Its adherents tend to remain in mainline congregations, while faulting "ordinary" Christians in their churches for a lack of spiritual zeal.

Many Christians have looked skeptically at the charismatic movement. Yet the zeal and excitement of charismatics catch our attention. We can't help but wonder if perhaps we are lacking something or leaving unused exciting gifts of the Spirit.

Background

The Scriptures indicate that each believer receives at least one spiritual gift. "To each one the manifestation of the Spirit is given for the common good. All these [spiritual gifts] are the work of one and the same Spirit, and he gives them to each one, just as he determines" (1 Corinthians 12:7,11).

There are numerous gifts—all coming from the undeserved love of God. There is, therefore, no reason—or right—for any believer to feel superior or more important than another. "Just as each of us has one body with many members, and these members do not all have the same function, so in Christ we who are many form one body, and each member belongs to all the others. We have different gifts, according to the grace given us" (Romans 12:4-6). The Spirit doles out gifts as he sees fit so that the body of Christ is healthy and functioning properly.

The Spirit gives his gifts with the intention that they be used to benefit others. "Each one should use whatever gift he has received to serve others, faithfully administering God's grace in its various forms" (1 Peter 4:10).

Before defining what spiritual gifts are, let's look at a few things they are not.

- Spiritual gifts are not essential to being a Christian. Faith, not charismatic gifts, makes a Christian. It is wrong to expect all Christians to have specific gifts, such as the ability to speak in tongues. The Spirit's gifts are given in differing amounts and combinations as he sees fit.

- Spiritual gifts are not merely natural talents. Christians and non-Christians alike have natural talents. Spiritual gifts are bestowed only upon Christians.

- Spiritual gifts are different from responsibilities. All Christians have responsibilities to serve, exhort, teach, give, witness, show mercy, grow in knowledge and wisdom, and so forth. To some the Spirit has given a special aptitude or *charisma* for carrying out those responsibilities.

- Spiritual gifts are not the same in every era or situation either. Rather, the Spirit gives his gifts for a purpose. He supplies whatever gifts are needed for the good of the church at a specific time and place according to its circumstances.

It's time for a definition. Spiritual gifts are *endowments of special abilities bestowed by the grace of God on individual Christians for the good of the church.* In other words, spiritual gifts are talents or aptitudes through which the Holy Spirit equips believers for spiritual service.

Listing of gifts

Four lists of spiritual gifts are given in the New Testament (Romans 12:6-8; 1 Corinthians 12:8-10; 1 Corinthians 12:28; Ephesians 4:11). Some gifts occur in more than one list. Prophecy or prophet, for example, appears in all four listings; teaching/teacher in three; miracles in two. Other gifts, such as evangelist, exhortation, and giving, appear only once. In addition to the lists just mentioned, Peter speaks of "various forms" of gifts and then points to speaking and serving as two general categories (1 Peter 4:10,11). We should not imagine that these lists are exhaustive. There certainly are other gifts, such as gifts of music, which are not specifically mentioned.

We can organize the listed gifts in the following manner:

FOUNDATIONAL GIFTS	CONFIRMATORY GIFTS
Prophet Apostle Discernment	Miracles Healing Speaking in Tongues Interpretation of Tongues

CONTINUING GIFTS	
SPEAKING	*SERVING*
Evangelist Pastor Teacher/Teaching Exhortation Word of Wisdom Word of Knowledge	Serving Giving Leadership Administration Showing Mercy/Helps Faith

In the rest of this chapter we will look at special gifts the Spirit has given in the past but no longer seems to be giving. In the next chapter we will look at spiritual gifts he still gives for the good of the church.

Foundational gifts

Prophet

We can define the spiritual gift of prophet this way: the divine endowment to receive and speak forth truth received by direct revelation from God.

A *prophet* is one who speaks for God. In the days before the completion of the Bible, prophets routinely received revelations directly from God. Among the divine messages they faithfully delivered to the people were predictions regarding the future. The Bible prescribes two tests of a true prophet. First, his message won't contradict God's revealed will (Isaiah 8:20). Second, all his predictions will come true (Deuteronomy 18:22).

Through the prophets in the Old Testament times, God gave his church his Word, which he moved the prophets to record in the 39 books of the Old Testament. "In the past God spoke to our forefathers through the prophets" (Hebrews 1:1). The New Testament church in its early years was also blessed with prophets (Acts 11:27; 13:1; 1 Corinthians 14:29; Ephesians 4:11). The prophets were the preachers of their day. While their work continues in the preachers who proclaim the truth of the Bible today, prophets who received direct revelations were gifts for the time before the completion of the Bible.

Apostle

The gift of being an *apostle* was given to a very limited number of men to act with God-given power and to speak with God-given authority by virtue of personal knowledge of Christ and direct revelation of the Spirit.

Apostle comes from the Greek verb *apostello*, which means "to send out." Its noun derivative, *apostolos*, was used as a nautical term in classical Greek. It meant "a vessel sent on a mission." *Apostolos* came to mean "a person sent out as an envoy." Our Lord Jesus chose 13 men to be his apostles: the 12 disciples (who remained 12 in number because Matthias replaced Judas Iscariot) and Paul. One of the qualifications of an apostle was that he had "been with us the whole time the Lord Jesus went in and out among us" (Acts 1:21). The Lord Jesus himself made an exception to that rule in the case of Paul. The apostles were given special powers to back up the message they were sent out to proclaim: "The things that mark an apostle—signs, wonders and miracles—were done among you with great perseverance" (2 Corinthians 12:12). The apostles were Jesus' specially chosen ambassadors to be the foundational teachers of the New Testament church and to proclaim the gospel to the world through their preaching and through the Scriptures they wrote.

Today no one can meet the qualifications of apostleship, in particular being an eyewitness of Jesus' ministry. Moreover, special revelations are no longer needed since the Scriptures are complete, containing everything necessary "for teaching, rebuking, correcting and training in righteousness, so that the man of God may be thoroughly equipped for every good work" (2 Timothy 3:16,17). We conclude, therefore, that the Holy Spirit no longer gives apostles to the modern-day church.

The prophets and apostles were foundational gifts essential for establishing the church. They faithfully carried out their assignment. The holy Christian church stands today, "built on the foundation of the apostles and prophets" (Ephesians 2:20), who continue to speak to us through the Scriptures.

Discernment

The listing of the Spirit's special gifts includes *discernment* or "distinguishing between spirits" (1 Corinthians 12:10). Before the Bible was completed and everyone agreed which books belonged in it, that foundational gift was also needed.

> Two or three prophets should speak, and the others should weigh carefully what is said. (1 Corinthians 14:29)

> Do not treat prophecies with contempt. Test everything. Hold on to the good. Avoid every kind of evil. (1 Thessalonians 5:20-22)

The spiritual gift of discernment was the ability to evaluate the message of one who claimed to have received a revelation or a prophecy from God. Through this spiritual gift the believer could determine if the message came from the Holy Spirit or if its source was the speaker's own human spirit or even an evil spirit.

All Christians need to "test the spirits to see whether they are from God, because many false prophets have gone out into the world" (1 John 4:1). Today the Holy Spirit enlightens us and equips us for such testing through the Scriptures. The gift of supernatural powers of discernment seems to have been foundational, however. Need for it ceased once the Scriptures were available as the norm for Spirit-enlightened testing.

Confirmatory gifts

Of all the Spirit's gifts, the confirmatory gifts arouse the most interest and attention. Miracles, healings, and speaking in tongues are spectacular in nature. Moreover, Pentecostals and charismatics claim to be receiving these gifts today. If these gifts are still available to believers, we would like a piece of the action too!

Miracles

Among the spiritual gifts mentioned in the New Testament is *miraculous powers*, through which the Holy Spirit provides "workers of miracles" (1 Corinthians 12:28). A miracle is an act of supernatural power through which God overturns the normal course of nature. A miracle elicits awe and wonder and serves as a sign to authenticate the worker as one backed by God. The gift of miracles, then, is the ability to perform supernatural acts that show God's approval of the message or messenger.

Healing

Healing is really a subcategory of miracles. The person with the gift of healing served as an intermediary through whom God intervened with supernatural power to cure illness and restore health. Jesus performed numerous miracles of healing; 25 are specifically mentioned in the four gospels. Jesus' healings were instantaneous and complete.[27] When he attempted a healing, he had a one hundred percent success rate.

Jesus encouraged his believers to preach the good news to all creation with this promise: "Signs will accompany those who believe: In my name . . . they will place their hands on sick people, and they will get well" (Mark 16:17,18).

It seems that in the early days of the New Testament church, the Spirit made known in some way when a miraculous sign was in order, for not even the apostles had the power to heal everyone or the option of healing whenever they wanted. Paul, for example, wrote regarding one of his faithful coworkers, "I left Trophimus sick in Miletus" (2 Timothy 4:20). Rather than heal Timothy's chronic stomach condition, Paul advised him regarding proper health care (1 Timothy 5:23). Moreover, Paul's prayers for his own healing were not answered with a miracle. Rather, the Lord helped Paul accept his affliction and see God's good purpose for it: "Three times I pleaded with the Lord to take it [the thorn in my flesh] away from me. But he said to me, 'My grace is sufficient for you, for my power is made perfect in weakness.' Therefore I will boast all the more gladly about my weaknesses, so that Christ's power may rest on me" (2 Corinthians 12:8,9).

Miracles and healings were given at critical periods in biblical history. They were especially evident at the time of the exodus, during the perilous times of the prophets, in Jesus' lifetime, and in the beginning years of the New Testament church. Those were pivotal times when God was intervening in world history. At those times God determined that his presence and the authenticity of his message needed to be demonstrated beyond a shadow of a doubt. The gifts of miracles and healing were his way of proving that.

God remains almighty. If he chooses to grant miracles and miraculous healings today, he is fully capable of doing so. The evidence, however, indicates that such gifts served confirmatory purposes at pivotal points in history. Now the Bible is readily available; now the church is solidly established. Supernatural wonders to confirm God's presence in the church or his backing of the gospel message are no longer needed.

Today we do best when we take our needs directly to the Lord in prayer, confident that "the prayer of a righteous man is powerful and effective" (James 5:16). Why look for a person with the gift of miraculous healing power when you can go straight to the power source? In answer to your prayers, God may choose to grant a miraculous healing also.

Speaking in tongues and interpretation of tongues

The confirmatory gifts that get the most attention are *speaking in tongues* and *the interpretation of tongues*. The gift of speaking in tongues is the special ability to speak in another language, one not previously known by the speaker. Interpretation of tongues is the miraculous ability to interpret the words of a person speaking in tongues.

Glossolalia is another term for speaking in tongues; it comes from the Greek words *glossa* (tongue) and *lalia* (speaking). On Pentecost the Holy Spirit enabled the apostles to speak in foreign languages they had not previously known. "Parthians, Medes and Elamites; residents of Mesopotamia, Judea and Cappadocia, Pontus and Asia, Phrygia and Pamphylia, Egypt and the parts of Libya near Cyrene; visitors from Rome (both Jews and converts to Judaism); Cretans and Arabs—we hear them declaring the wonders of God in our own tongues!" (Acts 2:9-11). The gift was the ability to communicate the gospel in recognizable foreign languages to individuals who spoke those languages. It was clear evidence that God backed the message of Jesus that was being preached.

Much of the confusion regarding this gift rests with the English translation "tongues." The KJV clouds things even more when it adds the word "unknown" (1 Corinthians 14:2,4,13,14,19,27). When the KJV talks of "unknown tongues," it leaves the impression that some bizarre, unintelligible language was being spoken. The New International Version correctly offers "languages" as an alternate translation for "tongues." There would be less confusion if our English Bibles consistently translated this gift as the ability to "speak in languages they hadn't known before."

In addition to Pentecost, the book of Acts tells of two other times when the miraculous gift of speaking in tongues was given (10:44-47; 19:1-7). In the first instance, Peter preached to Cornelius, a Gentile, and God showed his approval by enabling the Gentiles to speak in tongues. Jewish Christians wondered, Can Gentiles be saved? Does God approve of going to the non-Jews? God gave his answer. He confirmed his approval through a miraculous sign. Notice that the tongues were recognizable languages, just like on Pentecost, for Peter comments, "God gave them *the same gift as he gave us*, who believed in the Lord Jesus Christ" (11:17).

In the second case, Paul preached in Ephesus to believers who knew nothing about the Holy Spirit. Was Paul telling them the truth? God said a clear yes by confirming Paul's preaching. The men, about 12 in number, were baptized, and "the Holy Spirit came on them, and they spoke in tongues" (19:6).

In Corinth things had gotten out of hand. Apparently those who spoke in tongues were breaking forth in ecstatic speech, which no one present understood and which, therefore, served no good in communicating the gospel. Paul wrote to instruct them about the proper use of tongues: "In the church I would rather speak five intelligible words to instruct others than ten thousand words in a tongue" (1 Corinthians 14:19). Moreover, tongues serve no purpose in the church without someone to interpret:

"If there is no interpreter, the speaker should keep quiet in the church and speak to himself and God" (verse 28).

A study of the Scriptures leads to the conclusion that tongues were like the miracles and healing we mentioned earlier. All three were confirmatory gifts, given by God at crucial times and under extraordinary circumstances to establish his New Testament church and authenticate the gospel of Jesus. The message was new and subject to the legitimate question "How can we be sure you are telling the truth?" The confirmatory gifts were God's way of showing his approval of what was being said in his name. While God can still give the gift of languages, we do not have reason to expect it nor need for it. What's more, there is no promise in the Bible that this gift will continue in the church until the end of time.

Though we do not base doctrine upon church history, it is interesting to note how speaking in tongues has fared in the history of the church. It is a historical fact that speaking in tongues for all practical purposes ended with the death of the apostles. By A.D. 400 the church father Augustine spoke of speaking in tongues as something that was gone from the church. Speaking in tongues was practiced sporadically only in radical fringe elements of the church throughout the entire period from A.D. 100 to 1900. This disappearance of speaking in tongues supports the idea that it was a confirmatory gift given to the church only at the time of the apostles.

When did the current phenomenon emerge? Modern-day speaking in tongues often traces its beginning to January 1, 1901, when Miss Agnes Ozman spoke in what she claimed was a Chinese tongue at the College of Bethel Bible School in Topeka, Kansas. It is noteworthy that she spoke in tongues only after anguished longings and prayers for the gift. This reception is in striking contrast with the tongues of the Bible, which always fell on people unexpectedly and without people seeking them. From this humble beginning, speaking in tongues has spread around the world. Numerous Pentecostal denominations have arisen. The charismatic movement has also infiltrated many of the traditional Christian denominations.

We have much reason to challenge the role for tongues claimed by many modern-day Pentecostals and charismatics. Such individuals speak of a second baptism, a Spirit baptism, which is proven by the ability to speak in tongues. *The Statement of Fundamental Truths* of the Assemblies of God says, "The Baptism of believers in the Holy Ghost is witnessed by the initial physical sign of speaking with other tongues as the Spirit of God gives utterance (Acts 2:4)."[28] As the preceding quote illustrates, most Pentecostals believe that unless you have spoken in tongues, you have not yet been baptized in the Holy Spirit. We saw earlier in this book,[29] however, that baptism with water is the baptism of the Holy Spirit. Through that baptism we receive the Spirit, who gives us saving faith, and with faith come all the blessings God has planned for his children. God's ship is a one-class ship. There is not a tourist class for marginal, water-baptized Christians and a first class for Spirit-filled, tongues-speaking Christians.

Many modern-day charismatics regard speaking in tongues as the identifying mark of a true follower of Jesus. They establish fellowship ties on the basis of sharing that common experience. One's teaching on other Scriptural doctrines seems unimportant. The true mark of a God-pleasing church, however, is "teaching them to obey everything I have commanded you" (Matthew 28:20). And the true mark of a believer is holding to all the doctrines of the Bible. Where the Bible's truths are being falsely taught, it is doubtful the Holy Spirit is giving tongues to show his approval.

Some are convinced that the speaking in tongues in the contemporary charismatic movement is psychologically self-induced. Others point to the fact that this phenomenon is not limited to Christianity. Heathen religions in places like Africa make use of similar ecstatic speech. We know that the devil can lead false teachers to "perform great signs and miracles to deceive" (Matthew 24:24). While we do not question the sincerity of charismatics, we have reason to doubt what they are doing.

The Spirit can still give the ability to speak in a language one has not studied or previously known. We do not expect that spiritual gift to be ordinary or commonplace, however, since there is no promise in the Bible that it is to be received generally by Christians in every age. Even in the New Testament, it was comparatively rare. Certainly it is not something every Christian should expect to receive. Instead of craving the ability to speak in tongues, we will want to heed Paul's advice and place our emphasis on the clear proclamation of the Word: "If the trumpet does not sound a clear call, who will get ready for battle? So it is with you. Unless you speak intelligible words with your tongue, how will anyone know what you are saying? You will just be speaking into the air. . . . Since you are eager to have spiritual gifts, try to excel in gifts that build up the church" (1 Corinthians 14:8,9,12).

Foundational and confirmatory gifts today

The foundational and confirmatory gifts were spectacular, exciting, and essential for the time when they were given. In less spectacular ways those gifts continue to be supplied to God's church today. A form of the gift of prophecy continues in pastors who faithfully preach God's Word. Christians continue lovingly to share with the world the good news of Jesus and what he has done. Healing is granted in answer to prayer. Missionaries are given the ability to learn foreign languages and then communicate the gospel powerfully through them. Based on God's written Word, enlightened believers can discern divine truth from the devil's lies.

9

Continuing Gifts
for the Good of the Church

The church and the Bible are firmly established today. Spectacular foundational and confirmatory gifts are no longer necessary. Now the Holy Spirit concentrates on works that are outwardly less spectacular. He works inside people, changing and empowering them. He guides saints like you and me in building the kingdom of God and glorifying Jesus. With that goal in mind, the Spirit continues quietly to equip the saints "so that the body of Christ may be built up" (Ephesians 4:12).

In this chapter we will discuss the wide variety of continuing spiritual gifts the Spirit gives for the good of the church. God urges us, while we read, to think about how faithfully we are using the gifts he has given us. "Each one should use whatever gift he has received to serve others, faithfully administering God's grace in its various forms . . . so that in all things God may be praised through Jesus Christ" (1 Peter 4:10,11).

Speaking gifts

Evangelist

In Acts 8 we read about Philip the evangelist. He is best remembered for his one-on-one witnessing to the Ethiopian eunuch. Philip told the Ethiopian the good news about Jesus. Then at the Ethiopian's request, Philip baptized him. After this encounter Philip traveled on, preaching the gospel in all the towns along the way.

The Holy Spirit continues to supply *evangelists* like Philip. The evangelism gift is the spiritual gift of being able to present the gospel especially to those who are not yet believers. All Christians are to be witnesses of the gospel. Some, however, have a special knack for speaking to unbelievers and sharing the good news with them. That knack is a gift of the Spirit through which he draws people to faith and enlarges the kingdom of God.

Pastor

For the good of the church, the Holy Spirit continues to provide *shepherds*, who guide, comfort, protect, and nourish Jesus' sheep with the Word and sacraments. We usually call such men by the Latin word for shepherd, *pastors*. A pastor's call defines the flock of Christians he is to shepherd. Ordinarily he serves as spiritual leader of a local congregation. Pastors are placed over their flocks by the Holy Spirit. Paul tells the Ephesian leaders: "Keep watch over yourselves and all the flock of which the Holy Spirit has made you overseers. Be shepherds of the church of God, which he bought with his own blood" (Acts 20:28). Peter describes the shepherd's attitude toward the flock under his care: "Serving as overseers— not because you must, but because you are willing, as God wants you to be; not greedy for money, but eager to serve; not lording it over those entrusted to you, but being examples to the flock" (1 Peter 5:2,3). In addition to the pastor, other Christians may have a shepherding gift and be called by the congregation to assume ongoing responsibility for the spiritual welfare of another Christian or group of Christians. In most congregations elders serve such a role.

The Lord himself sets the perfect example of a shepherd, guiding, comforting, protecting and nourishing his sheep. "The Lord is my shepherd. . . . He guides me in paths of righteousness. . . . I will fear no evil, for you are with me; your rod and your staff, they comfort me. You prepare a table before me in the presence of my enemies" (Psalm 23:1,3-5).

Teachers/teaching

Teachers and the gift of teaching are also spiritual gifts. Teaching is the ability to explain clearly and apply effectively a truth. When that ability is used in communicating the truths of God's Word, it is a precious spiritual gift.

> A person with the gift of teaching will be marked by two characteristics. He will have a keen interest in the personal study of the Word and in the disciplines involved in studying the Scriptures. . . . Also he will have the capacity to communicate clearly the truths and applications of the Word so that others may learn and profit. After you have

heard a "teacher" teach, your response should be "I see what he means."[30]

"Go and make disciples . . . , baptizing . . . and teaching them to obey everything I have commanded you," Jesus said (Matthew 28:19,20). A quick perusal of the book of Acts shows the prominence of teaching:

> They [the believers in Jerusalem] devoted themselves to the apostles' teaching. (2:42)

> For a whole year Barnabas and Saul met with the church [at Antioch] and taught great numbers of people. (11:26)

> Paul stayed for a year and a half [in Corinth], teaching them the word of God. (18:11)

Psalm 78 speaks of the importance of teaching children:

> We will tell the next generation the praiseworthy deeds of the LORD, his power, and the wonders he has done. . . . He commanded our forefathers to teach their children, so the next generation would know them, even the children yet to be born, and they in turn would tell their children. Then they would put their trust in God and would not forget his deeds but would keep his commands. (verses 4-7)

Exhortation

In an earlier chapter we learned to call the Holy Spirit the Paraclete, the one who is called to our side to comfort and counsel us. The Paraclete blesses the church with "underparacletes." He gives a special ability to certain Christians to comfort and encourage others. This is the gift of *exhortation*. The apostle John gives an example of exhortation: "My dear children, I write this to you so that you will not sin. But if anybody does sin, we have one who speaks to the Father in our defense—Jesus Christ, the Righteous One" (1 John 2:1). Notice the relationship: "My dear children." John really cares for them and is truly concerned about them. Notice the admonition: "That you will not sin." Notice the comfort: "We have one who speaks to the Father in our defense."

Barnabas had the gift of exhortation. His name means "Son of Encouragement" (Acts 4:36). Barnabas joined Paul on the first missionary journey and served in a strong encouraging and supporting role. On that first journey the young man John Mark deserted Paul and returned home. John Mark could easily have been written off on the basis of that one moment of weakness—in fact, Paul seemed ready to give up on him. Barnabas, however, encouraged John Mark and took him along as his partner on the next trip (13:13; 15:37-39). John Mark went on to become the Mark who wrote one of the four gospels of the New Testament. We are all spiritually richer because of him and because Barnabas encouraged him.

Some Christians know how to exhort. They may not be directly involved in a project themselves, but they see the work that others are doing and encourage them to press forward. They have a knack for seeing when someone is hurting or becoming discouraged. They know how to give comfort and encouragement when it is really needed.

Word of wisdom and word of knowledge

"To one there is given through the Spirit the message of wisdom, to another the message of knowledge by means of the same Spirit" (1 Corinthians 12:8). The list of spiritual gifts includes *the message of wisdom* and *the message of knowledge*. Something special is meant here, different from the saving wisdom and knowledge all believers have.

Knowledge is the ability to grasp, organize, and retain facts. Wisdom is the ability to see the relevance and application of facts to specific situations. Knowledge is more theoretical in nature; wisdom, more practical. The message of knowledge, then, is the special ability to discover and communicate the truths God has revealed in his Word. The message of wisdom is the divine endowment to apply scriptural truths to specific needs and problems. Every congregation needs those who know the facts. Just as crucial are those who know how to apply God's truth correctly and with spiritual insight.

The spiritual gifts of evangelist, pastor, teacher, exhortation, knowledge, and wisdom are primarily speaking gifts. The Holy Spirit supplies these gifts to the Christian church to bring people to faith, strengthen them in faith, and guide, encourage, comfort and correct them. The Spirit gives speaking gifts so we can use them. Paul urges us, "Let the word of Christ dwell in you richly as you teach and admonish one another with all wisdom" (Colossians 3:16).

Serving gifts

The second major division of the continuing gifts of the Spirit for the good of the church is the serving gifts. These gifts emphasize deeds more than words. Often deeds, however, will set up opportunities for Christians to witness to the Savior, whose love motivates them to such good works.

We should note that every Christian is called upon to serve, give, help, or show mercy. In this section, however, we will be talking about those to whom the Holy Spirit gives a special gift or extraordinary strength for a particular form of service.

Serving

Paul lists *serving* as one of the Spirit's gifts (Romans 12:7). The gift of serving refers to the talent God gives to some to work faithfully and contentedly in a supportive role. The Greek word for service, *diakonia*, gives us the English word *deacon*. In Acts 6 we are told of the seven deacons who were elected to administer the daily distribution of food in the Jerusalem congregation. When the deacons took over that responsibility, the apostles were freed to give their attention to prayer and to the ministry of the Word.

Consider the example of Mary Magdalene. She became a follower of Jesus when he miraculously freed her by driving seven demons out of her. In gratitude for what Jesus had done for her, she found her greatest joy in following Jesus and ministering to his needs and those of the disciples (Luke 8:1-3). Her service and love were obvious in her willingness to carry out the embalming process on Jesus' dead body (Mark 16:1-3). Like Mary Magdalene, some Christians today are willing to serve in any capacity, no matter how menial, out of thankfulness for what Christ has done for them. They stuff bulletins, clean Communion ware, pull weeds, or wait on tables. Most times they don't even have to be asked. They see things that need to be done and just do them. They're not looking for a pat on the back; they simply want to serve the Lord in any way they can.

Giving

The gift of giving is the Spirit-worked willingness and cheerfulness to contribute one's material resources with extraordinary generosity. The Bible mentions for us some striking examples of those who excelled in the grace of *giving.* There was the widow who gave her last two copper coins (Mark 12:41-44). There were the believers in Jerusalem: "No one claimed that any of his possessions was his own, but they shared everything they had. There were no needy persons among them. For from time to time those who owned lands or houses sold them, brought the money from the sales and put it at the apostles' feet, and it was distributed to anyone as he had need" (Acts 4:32,34,35). There were the Macedonian Christians: "Out of the most severe trial, their overflowing joy and their extreme poverty welled up in rich generosity. For I testify that they gave as much as they were able, and even beyond their ability. Entirely on their own, they urgently pleaded with us for the privilege of sharing in this service to the saints" (2 Corinthians 8:2-4).

Leadership

Paul writes, "If it [one's gift] is leadership, let him govern diligently" (Romans 12:8). *Leadership* is the ability to oversee the work of the church with vision and by example in a manner that inspires others to follow. The Bible tells us that a leader in the church is to be a man of spiritual maturity, not a new convert. He is to manage well his own household. He is to be of good reputation within the church and outside it (1 Timothy 3:4,6,7). He leads by example, not lording it over those entrusted to him, but being an example to the flock (1 Peter 5:3).

Administration

The gift of *administration* (1 Corinthians 12:28) is closely akin to leadership. *Administration* is a nautical term in Greek. It refers to the helmsman of a ship, the one who steers the ship through the shoals, guides it on the course the ship's owner has determined, and brings it safely to its port of destination. In just this way an administrator in God's church guides the congregation on the course set by God in his Word and, in matters not determined by the Word, on the course set by the members of the congregation. One with a gift for administration can organize and carry through details. He also can delegate and motivate people.

Showing mercy/helps

The Bible abounds with examples of *showing mercy* and *giving help* (Romans 12:8; 1 Corinthians 12:28). Consider the Good Samaritan (Luke 10:25-37). Consider Jesus himself as he answered numerous calls for mercy and granted healing. The Bible describes God as one who is "rich in mercy" and who did something about our need by making us "alive with Christ" (Ephesians 2:4,5). Mercy is sympathy for another that shows itself not only in words, but also in helpful actions.

The spiritual gift of showing mercy or helping others is the ability to feel genuine compassion for suffering individuals and to translate that feeling into Christlike deeds that alleviate the suffering. Jesus wants every Christian to show kindness and love to others. We all know particular individuals, however, who have an extraordinary heart for the hurting and abound in kindness toward others. Such people are special gifts of the Holy Spirit.

Faith

"To one there is given . . . *faith* by the same Spirit" (1 Corinthians 12:8,9). We learned in an earlier chapter that saving faith is the Spirit's gift to all Christians. Therefore, Paul must be referring to something different here.

He gives an indication of what he has in mind a little later in 1 Corinthians, when he describes what is sometimes called heroic faith. There Paul speaks of "a faith that can move mountains" (13:2). This spiritual gift of heroic faith has been called Christian optimism. It is the ability to see something that needs to be done and believe that God will do it even if it looks impossible.

Silas is a man who exhibited such faith. On one occasion Paul and Silas were severely beaten and imprisoned at Philippi. Yet the two spent the night praying and singing praises to God (Acts 16:16-34). In Berea the crowds became agitated at Paul's preaching and rioted. Paul went on to Athens to escape the danger, but Silas remained there for some time, continuing the work (17:10-15). To this day there are Christians who are not discouraged by the mere fact that something appears difficult or impossible. They see opportunity where others see only opposition. They are the first to say "It can be done," rather than "It is impossible." They are visionaries—some would call them dreamers. But God uses the heroic faith of such people to lift the sights of his believers and move his church forward.

These are the special gifts mentioned in the New Testament. It can be said again that these listings are not necessarily exhaustive. There may be other gifts that the Holy Spirit gives to individual people for the common good. For example, one thinks of the gift of music, which has been so richly enjoyed in the church throughout its history. Surely it is a gift of the Holy Spirit when a believer composes or performs music that builds up other Christians and through music leads them to praise and glorify God. One also thinks of the gift of artistic talent. Just as the Holy Spirit equipped Bezalel and Oholiab for the work of building and decorating the tabernacle (Exodus 31:2-6), so the Holy Spirit raises up believers in our time to enrich the worship of the church with beautiful buildings and works of art.

Use of our spiritual gifts

The Holy Spirit continues to give out spiritual gifts to the church today. The application for us is twofold: confidence and encouragement.

We are confident that whatever the future may bring, the Spirit will see to it that the body of Christ has the necessary members and gifts. The necessary gifts may vary in different places at different times. Yet whatever the situation, God will provide what is needed "so that the body of Christ may be built up" (Ephesians 4:12).

The second application is encouragement to use our gifts. Part of the encouragement comes from inside us. The Holy Spirit plants interests in us. He gives us an inclination or a willingness to try a particular form of service to others. Part of the encouragement comes from without. The Holy Spirit places specific opportunities before us to use our gifts. Being asked to serve as a Sunday school teacher or a choir member, for example, may be the Spirit's way of calling us to a new form of service for which he has equipped us. A sick relative or a troubled coworker may be a call from the Spirit to try out our ability to show mercy or speak exhortation.

Making good use of God's gifts poses an ongoing challenge to our congregations. There is a story about a pastor who preached an especially effective sermon on using one's spiritual gifts. At the end of the sermon he called for volunteers who were willing to serve. A hundred men responded! Someone close to the pastor heard him mutter softly, "O God, how can I use a hundred ushers?" The point? Christians need to serve God with the talents the Spirit has given them. The congregation needs to manage that valuable pool of workers and skills—training its members for service and then helping them find meaningful opportunities to serve for the good of the church.

10

Preservation of the Saints

"He who stands firm to the end will be saved," Jesus promised (Matthew 24:13). The Christian's goal is to be among those who remain firm in saving faith to the end and thereafter enjoy the bliss of heaven. At the time of death, the believer wants to be able to echo the words of Saint Paul: "I have fought the good fight, I have finished the race, I have kept the faith. Now there is in store for me the crown of righteousness, which the Lord, the righteous Judge, will award to me on that day—and not only to me, but also to all who have longed for his appearing" (2 Timothy 4:7,8).

Every home has a collection of unfinished projects. There is the hope chest Father started for Mary that he hopes will be finished before her tenth wedding anniversary. There is the half-done quilt Mother began years ago. There is the model Johnny worked on so faithfully until the wing wouldn't fit right and he gave up in frustration. There are little Susie's half-painted artistic masterpieces. Some of those projects seemed like good ideas when we started them, but we lost interest once we found they were bigger jobs than we anticipated. Others remain good ideas; it's just that they never seem to make it to the top of the priority list. Some of our unfinished projects will get done eventually; others will never be completed.

Thank God that the Holy Spirit is no quitter. He leaves no projects unfinished. He completes what he starts. When the Spirit enters a heart and calls it to saving faith, he makes a pledge. He promises to continue working in the believer to keep him or her in that faith. The Holy Spirit keeps his promise! He preserves saints in the true faith. He brings them safely to their heavenly goal.

Warnings

Christians face very real danger as long as they live on this earth, however—the danger of losing their faith and salvation. "Once saved, always saved" is simply not true according to the Bible. It is possible to fall away from faith and be eternally lost. Saint Paul recalls tragedies that befell God's chosen people of the Old Testament because of God's judgment. Then he makes application to us of the New Testament: "These things happened to them as examples and were written down as warnings for us, on whom the fulfillment of the ages has come. So, if you think you are standing firm, be careful that you don't fall!" (1 Corinthians 10:11,12). Paul recognized the danger of falling away even for himself: "I beat my body and make it my slave so that after I have preached to others, I myself will not be disqualified for the prize" (9:27).

The Israelites were God's chosen people. If God's judgment cut off some of his chosen ones, certainly he will condemn us if we turn away from him: "They [some of the branches on God's olive tree] were broken off because of unbelief, and you stand by faith. Do not be arrogant, but be afraid. For if God did not spare the natural branches, he will not spare you either" (Romans 11:20,21). Notice what lies at the core of the danger. Arrogance leads to a fall—arrogance that feels no need for watchfulness and no need for the faith-strengthening tools God has given.

Peter fell disastrously on Maundy Thursday due to arrogant self-trust. "Even if all fall away on account of you, I never will," Peter insisted (Matthew 26:33), even though Jesus had just warned, "This very night you will all fall away on account of me" (verse 31). Jesus warned him, "I tell you, Peter, before the rooster crows today, you will deny three times that you know me" (Luke 22:34). Instead of heeding the warning, Peter's arrogance continued: "Even if I have to die with you, I will never disown you" (Matthew 26:35). Peter believed that he was capable of greater faith and greater faithfulness than his fellow disciples.

God's law warns of the danger of sin and unbelief. That warning is also meant for believers. A whole array of things can cause believers to lose their faith:

- *Persecution* such as the implied or expressed ridicule that is directed against the Bible's teachings in public education and public policy.

- *False doctrine and false teachers*—Jesus warned that especially in the last times, "many false prophets will appear and deceive many people" (Matthew 24:11).

- *Spiritual starvation,* which results from neglect of the means by which the Spirit preserves faith. Deprive the body of food and it will starve. Deprive the soul of spiritual nutrition and it also will starve.

- *Self-righteousness,* which shifts one's trust from the grace of God to one's own works or strength.

- *Humanistic pride,* which refuses to submit to the authority of God's Word.

- *Love of the world*—when Christians become so concerned with the affairs of this world that the needs of the soul are forgotten.

- *Willful sins against one's conscience* for as the Lutheran Confessions say, "we should not imagine a kind of faith . . . that could coexist and co-persist with a wicked intention to sin and to act contrary to one's conscience."[31]

The Lord Jesus warned strongly: "I tell you, every sin and blasphemy will be forgiven men, but the blasphemy against the Spirit will not be forgiven. Anyone who . . . speaks against the Holy Spirit will not be forgiven, either in this age or in the age to come" (Matthew 12:31,32).[32] This is called the unforgivable sin, or the sin against the Holy Spirit. Since no one can call Jesus Lord except by the Holy Spirit (1 Corinthians 12:3), it is impossible to repent and come to faith if one consciously and deliberately rejects the working of the Spirit and drives him from the heart.

The sin against the Holy Spirit is not blasphemy or unbelief that flows from spiritual blindness. Such blasphemy is every sinful human being's natural reaction to the Spirit. The Spirit is the one who changes rejection of God into faith. The sin against the Holy Spirit is committed only after the Spirit has clearly revealed the truth to the sinner. It is the malicious rejection of the gospel by one who through the working of the Holy Spirit had been fully convinced of its divine truth. In other words, it is turning away from faith by hardening one's heart to the Spirit's work and message. We see this clearly in the letter to the Hebrews, where a detailed description is given of those who cannot be brought back to repentance:

> It is impossible for those who have once been enlightened, who have tasted the heavenly gift, who have shared in the Holy Spirit, who have tasted the goodness of the word of God and the powers of the coming age, if they fall away, to be brought back to repentance, because to their loss they are crucifying the Son of God all over again and subjecting him to public disgrace. (6:4-6)

There is a comfort for those who are troubled that they may have committed the sin against the Holy Spirit. As long as one is worried about it, one has not committed it. Those who have slammed the door on the Spirit have no concern or regard whatsoever for their spiritual state.

Assurances

Humans can destroy life. They cannot create or preserve life, however. In a similar way, while humans have the power to defect from faith, they are not able to achieve their own perseverance in the faith. God must preserve faith and cause it to grow. And that is what God has promised to do.

To the Philippians Paul writes of "being confident of this, that he who began a good work in you will carry it on to completion until the day of Christ Jesus" (1:6).

Peter speaks of the Christian's "inheritance that can never perish, spoil or fade—kept in heaven for you, who through faith are shielded by God's power until the coming of the salvation that is ready to be revealed in the last time" (1 Peter 1:4,5).

Jesus himself promises this regarding his sheep: "I give them eternal life, and they shall never perish; no one can snatch them out of my hand. My Father, who has given them to me, is greater than all; no one can snatch them out of my Father's hand" (John 10:28,29).

Paul assured the Thessalonians: "May your whole spirit, soul and body be kept blameless at the coming of our Lord Jesus Christ. The one who calls you is faithful and he will do it" (1 Thessalonians 5:23,24). Again Paul said, "The Lord is faithful, and he will strengthen and protect you from the evil one" (2 Thessalonians 3:3). God takes salvation out of the believer's weak, helpless hands and places it into his gracious, almighty hands.

The Holy Spirit keeps us in the faith through his tools, the means of grace. The gospel of Christ is "the power of God for the salvation of everyone who believes" (Romans 1:16). That gospel, the good news of Jesus and what he has done for us, is found in the Bible, in Baptism, and in Holy Communion. Through the gospel in these powerful tools, the Holy Spirit preserves our faith and fortifies us to withstand the assaults that Satan sends to rob us of our salvation.

An important aside is the fact that the Spirit also preserves the Holy Scriptures so that no one can destroy their saving power. The Spirit did not inspire the Scriptures only to let their message be lost through copyists' errors, lost manuscripts, or heretics' attempts to alter the text. No, the Spirit has preserved the Bible—some parts for 3,400 years now. He has kept it from being distorted by deletions, additions, or mistakes. The Spirit continues to see to it that "[God's] word is truth" (John 17:17). He makes sure that "the word of the Lord stands forever" (1 Peter 1:25).

The Spirit also preserves faith by gathering believers into congregations so they may encourage and build up one another. In the days after Pentecost the Bible reports of the first Christians, "Every day they continued to meet together in the temple courts" (Acts 2:46). We live much closer to the day of judgment. Meeting to encourage one another is more important now than ever before: "Let us not give up meeting together, as some are in the habit of doing, but let us encourage one another—and all the more as you see the Day approaching" (Hebrews 10:25).

Through words of warning when needed and words of encouragement when appropriate, Christians become the Spirit's agents to help preserve one another in the faith: "See to it, brothers, that none of you has a sinful, unbelieving heart that turns away from the living God. But encourage one another daily, as long as it is called Today, so that none of you may be hardened by sin's deceitfulness" (Hebrews 3:12,13). What a blessing when God can commend a congregation as he did the Thessalonians: "Encourage one another and build each other up, just as in fact you are doing" (1 Thessalonians 5:11).

The Bible warns that trials will come: "We must go through many hardships to enter the kingdom of God" (Acts 14:22). Jesus called those hardships crosses: "If anyone would come after me, he must deny himself and take up his cross and follow me" (Mark 8:34). A cross is whatever a Christian must endure because of faith. Crosses may come in the form of the suffering, insults, persecution, and hatred we encounter because we live for Jesus in a sinful, ungodly world. Crosses may be the self-denial when we willingly forego certain luxuries and even necessities for the glory of Christ and the good of others. Sometimes we will forego things because they are sinful; sometimes simply because our Christian stewardship says there is a better use for that time or money. Our crosses will include the daily struggle with sin all of us wage within ourselves.

The Holy Spirit stands by as our Paraclete to help us bear our crosses. Moreover, he uses them for our spiritual good. Crosses can serve to keep us humble and close to our Lord. Crosses can bring us to our knees in more frequent and fervent prayer. Crosses can turn our thoughts away from earthly matters and focus them on things spiritual and eternal. Crosses also can help strengthen our faith and confidence regarding the future, for we learn to say from personal experience, "I can do everything through him [Christ] who gives me strength" (Philippians 4:13). Even in the severest trials, believers know that in the hands of almighty God, their salvation is absolutely secure.

As another part of his work of sanctification, the Holy Spirit works in us to make us more faithful in prayer. Moreover, when words fail us, when we are not certain just what to ask, when we cannot find the right way to express our feelings and inner needs, we have one who prays for us:

> The Spirit helps us in our weakness. We do not know what we ought to pray for, but the Spirit himself intercedes for us with groans that words cannot express. And he who searches our hearts knows the mind of the Spirit, because the Spirit intercedes for the saints in accordance with God's will. (Romans 8:26,27)

A congregation was worshiping when the electricity to the organ failed. An electrician was hastily summoned,

and he discovered the cause of the trouble almost immediately. It could be fixed quite quickly, so he scribbled a note
to deliver to the pastor. After reading the note, the pastor
informed the congregation: "After the prayer the power
will be on." In a similar way Christian prayer brings the
power of God down from above. We can accept as a general truism this statement: "Much prayer, much power. Little prayer, little power."

The Holy Scriptures promise that the Spirit, who calls
us to faith, will preserve us in that faith until we arrive
safely in heaven. We do not rely on our own spiritual
strength. Rather, we rest our confidence and certainty on
divine promises like this one:

> Who shall separate us from the love of Christ? Shall trou-
> ble or hardship or persecution or famine or nakedness or
> danger or sword? . . . No, in all these things we are more
> than conquerors through him who loved us. For I am con-
> vinced that neither death nor life, neither angels nor
> demons, neither the present nor the future, nor any pow-
> ers, neither height nor depth, nor anything else in all cre-
> ation, will be able to separate us from the love of God that
> is in Christ Jesus our Lord. (Romans 8:35,37-39)

A dilemma

This brings us to the horns of a dilemma. The Scriptures
contain strong warnings of the danger of losing our faith
and beautiful assurances that the Holy Spirit will preserve
us in saving faith. In fact, at times the Bible gives warnings
and assurances side by side in the very same passage. The
following are two examples:

> If you think you are standing firm, be careful that you
> don't fall! [Warning.] No temptation has seized you
> except what is common to man. And God is faithful; he

will not let you be tempted beyond what you can bear. But when you are tempted, he will also provide a way out so that you can stand up under it. [Assurance.] (1 Corinthians 10:12,13)

Your enemy the devil prowls around like a roaring lion looking for someone to devour. Resist him, standing firm in the faith. [Warning.] . . . And the God of all grace, who called you to his eternal glory in Christ, after you have suffered a little while, will himself restore you and make you strong, firm and steadfast. To him be the power for ever and ever. [Assurance.] (1 Peter 5:8-11)

Is there a contradiction here? It seems so. For in the same passages we are both warned of the real danger of falling and assured that God will not let us fall. To resolve the seeming conflict, we need only recall our needs as sinner-saints. We are prone to self-confidence, and therefore we need the warnings. We can easily become discouraged and be led to despair, and therefore we need the promises.

In the warnings and the assurances we see again law and gospel. Our old sinful nature needs to hear the law as a warning against worldly security and self-confidence. On the other hand, our new Christian nature trusts the gospel and its gracious promise of divine preservation.

Troubles come when we misapply the law and gospel. We fall into serious spiritual danger when we tell our sinful nature: "Don't worry about sin and Satan. God forgives." We fall into self-righteousness and serious false doctrine when we tell our new nature: "You can be assured of salvation if you do this or that." Our sinful nature needs the warnings of the law lest we grow careless or indifferent. Our Christian nature needs the comfort and assurances of the gospel lest we needlessly worry or fear.

On the job to the end

In Luther's explanation to the Third Article we confess: "On the Last Day he [the Spirit] will raise me and all the dead and give eternal life to me and all believers in Christ. This is most certainly true." The work of the Holy Spirit does not end until that day when all the saints stand safely in heaven, to be "with the Lord forever" (1 Thessalonians 4:17). It may come as a surprise that resurrecting our bodies is work done by the Holy Spirit. The Scriptures, however, speak of the Spirit's role: "If the Spirit of him who raised Jesus from the dead is living in you, he who raised Christ from the dead will also give life to your mortal bodies through his Spirit, who lives in you" (Romans 8:11). Actually, as this passage shows, the resurrection of our bodies is another of those divine tasks in which all three members of the Trinity have a part.

The promise that the Spirit will preserve us in the faith comforts us as we face death. Consider Stephen, when he stood before the angry mob preparing to stone him to death:

> Stephen, full of the Holy Spirit, looked up to heaven and saw the glory of God, and Jesus standing at the right hand of God. "Look," he said, "I see heaven open and the Son of Man standing at the right hand of God." While they were stoning him, Stephen prayed, "Lord Jesus, receive my spirit." Then he fell on his knees and cried out, "Lord, do not hold this sin against them." When he had said this, he fell asleep. (Acts 7:55,56,59,60)

We all hope that the circumstances surrounding our deaths will be better than those Stephen endured. As believers we can be confident, however, that, whatever the circumstances of our deaths, we too will be "full of the Holy Spirit" (Acts 7:55). The Spirit, who keeps saints in the faith to the end, will also comfort and strengthen them at death with the glorious hope of heaven.

Pope Paul VI, as he contemplated his impending death, said, "The fear of God's judgment at the moment of death is always present and full of mystery."[33] That seems to be a sad confession and also an indictment of Roman Catholic theology. The pope admitted fear of God's judgment and implied an uncertainty ("mystery") of what it held in store for him. What a sad admission. The gospel clearly says, "Whoever believes in the Son *has* eternal life" (John 3:36). True, our old sinful nature fears God's judgment. True, because we remain imperfect, our faith is not as strong and confident as it could be. True, doubts and anxieties come because of Satan's tempting. But the Holy Spirit has caused our new nature to know the gospel promise and believe it. That Spirit will be by our side as we pass through death's valley, too. He will hold the gospel before our dying eyes. Through it he will make us certain and unafraid. Confidence in the face of death is another of the Spirit's supernatural gifts.

As the days grow more evil and the end of this world approaches, the Holy Spirit will sustain the church also. "When the going gets tough, the tough get going," according to the old saying. We can be certain the Spirit's presence and power will be felt in increasing amounts as the end nears. He will make Jesus' claim on Maundy Thursday also true on the Last Day: "I have not lost one of those you gave me" (John 18:9).

The Spirit teaches us to pray for Jesus' return. After showing John the tumultuous events of the end times and the triumphant return of Jesus to gather his believers, the Spirit inspired John to end the book of Revelation with prayer. John recorded for us the prayer the Spirit teaches the saints to say: "Amen. Come, Lord Jesus" (22:20). "Amen"—that's the Spirit at work in us. We confess that what the Bible says about our Savior and his return is true. "Come"—that's also the Spirit at work in us. He teaches us to long for Jesus' arrival and eagerly pray for that day when we will enjoy the Spirit's gift of life to the full.

11

The Honor He Is Due

The Scriptures encourage us to glorify God, adding our voices to those of the angels in heaven and the saints of all ages: "Holy, holy, holy is the LORD Almighty; the whole earth is full of his glory" (Isaiah 6:3). As full God and an equal partner in the Trinity, the Holy Spirit is worthy of such divine honor, praise, and worship. God's people, therefore, sincerely desire to bring him the honor he is due.

Honoring him in our worship

Is the Holy Spirit slighted by the Christians of our day? Some answer yes. In fact, underlying the charismatic movement is the accusation that most churches do not

give the Spirit the honor and prominence he is due. A
brief look at worship in Lutheran churches, however, will
prove the error of such charges. The Holy Spirit is not forgotten. In fact, he has a prominent place in the worship
life of Christian people. To illustrate this, let's look briefly
at the Common Service in *Christian Worship: A Lutheran
Hymnal* (pages 15-25).

We honor the Spirit when we respect—and use—the
Word he inspired. "All Scripture is God-breathed and is
useful for teaching, rebuking, correcting and training in
righteousness, so that the man of God may be thoroughly
equipped for every good work" (2 Timothy 3:16,17). The
Spirit gave the Bible with the intention that it be a useful
tool for our lives. We honor him when we show apprecia-
tion for his book by using it to instruct and discipline ourselves so we mature in faith and godly living. Regular
attendance at worship is one of the ways to respect and use
the Bible.

The Spirit's means of grace are the heart and core of
Lutheran worship. The Common Service centers around
the reading of the Word (three lessons and a psalm) and
the study of the Word (the sermon). The sacraments sur-
round the Word. Holy Baptism, when it is administered,
opens the service. On Communion Sundays, the Lord's
Supper occupies a major portion of the service.

The Lutheran liturgical service gives the Holy Spirit a
prominent place, equal with the Father and the Son. We
invoke the Spirit's presence as we begin the service: "In the
name of the Father and of the Son and of the Holy Spirit"
(page 15). We draw on his authority and power as the pastor speaks the absolution: "I forgive you all your sins in the
name of the Father and of the Son and of the Holy Spirit"

(page 16). When we join to praise the Lord for the forgiveness he has given, we glorify the Spirit for his part: "You only, O Christ, with the Holy Spirit, are most high in the glory of God the Father" (page 17). Both the Nicene Creed and the Apostles' Creed confess our faith in the Holy Spirit. The Nicene Creed goes into considerable detail: "We believe in the Holy Spirit, the Lord, the giver of life, who proceeds from the Father and the Son, who in unity with the Father and the Son is worshiped and glorified, who has spoken through the prophets" (page 19). At the conclusion of the sermon, we pray for the Spirit's help to believe and put into practice what we have just heard: "Create in me a clean heart, O God, and renew a right spirit within me. Cast me not away from your presence, and take not your Holy Spirit from me. Restore unto me the joy of your salvation, and uphold me with your free Spirit" (page 20).

A study of the prayers used in the service shows that the Holy Spirit gets his share of mention there too. Some of the prayers are addressed to him directly. Others, such as the closing prayer for the service, ask that the Spirit be sent into our lives: "Almighty God, grant to your Church the Holy Spirit" (page 25). And then there is the regular ending for nearly all the prayers: "Through Jesus Christ, our Lord, who lives and reigns with you and the Holy Spirit, one God, now and forever" (pages 24,25).

The Spirit plays a prominent role in the hymns we sing too. Martin Luther gave us an excellent example in his great Pentecost hymn:

> Come, Holy Ghost, God and Lord!
>   May all your graces be outpoured
> On each believer's mind and heart;
>   Your fervent love to them impart.

Lord, by the brightness of your light
    In holy faith your church unite
From ev'ry land and ev'ry tongue;
    This to your praise, O Lord our God, be sung:
Alleluia! Alleluia!

Come, holy Light, Guide divine,
    And cause the Word of life to shine.
Teach us to know our God aright
    And call him Father with delight.
From ev'ry error keep us free;
    Let none but Christ our Master be
That we in living faith abide,
    In him, our Lord, with all our might confide.
Alleluia! Alleluia! (CW 176:1,2)

Does the Lutheran church slight the Holy Spirit? The answer is an emphatic no! In the liturgical service of the Lutheran church, the Spirit and his tools enjoy proper prominence. Of course, the Spirit is slighted if an individual fails to pay attention to the service each week.

Honoring him in the church year

In addition to his prominence in our worship, the Spirit is honored by one of the three major festivals of the church year. Pentecost is the Holy Spirit's holiday. It recalls what he did in Jerusalem that first Pentecost and assures us of his continuing work today. Pentecost goes back into Old Testament times. It was also called the Feast of Harvest, the Feast of Weeks, or the Day of Firstfruits. It celebrated the completion of the grain harvest. On Pentecost the firstfruits of the wheat harvest were presented as a thankoffering to the Lord. The Holy Spirit chose this day to become the birthday of the Christian church (Acts 2). On the first Pentecost three thousand people were converted and gathered into the first congregation. These converts were the firstfruits of the great spiritual harvest, which the Holy Spirit has been gathering ever since. As we commemorate Pentecost each year, we are grateful that the power of that same Holy Spirit has brought us into Christ's church.

We must admit that in contrast to Christmas and Easter, this third major festival attracts little attention. People in general show little interest in it. In fact, many churchgoers wouldn't even realize it was Pentecost if the pastor and church bulletin didn't remind them. On the other hand, half of the church year is counted as the Sundays after Pentecost. This long season, up to 24 Sundays a year, focuses on Spirit-produced spiritual growth. The relative quietness of the typical Pentecost festival and the half year of steady teaching and growth during the Sundays after Pentecost are actually a fitting tribute to the Spirit. Quietly, steadily, faithfully the Spirit works through the preaching and teaching of the Word and the administration of the sacraments, which all center in Christ. As the Spirit works through Word and sacraments, he focuses our attention primarily on Christ, just as Jesus said he would (John 16:14).

Honoring him with our lives

Christian parents receive their greatest joy from seeing their children believe in Jesus and live godly lives. In a similar way the Spirit rejoices when his children, the saints, trust in the Savior and do all things in the name of the Lord Jesus, giving thanks to God the Father through him. We praise and honor the Spirit, therefore, when we place our trust in Jesus and live our lives for him. Such faith and living show that the Spirit's efforts have not been wasted on us, but rather are respected and appreciated by us.

The Bible encourages us to honor the Spirit in our lives each day: "Do not grieve the Holy Spirit of God, with whom you were sealed for the day of redemption" (Ephesians 4:30). The context of this verse warns against falsehood, unwholesome talk, anger, and every form of malice. Such things sadden the Holy Spirit. The text then tells the way to honor the Spirit: "Be kind and compassionate to one another, forgiving each other, just as in Christ God forgave you. Be imitators of God, therefore, as dearly loved children and live a life of love, just as Christ loved us and gave himself up for us" (4:32–5:2).

A phenomenal amount of potential electric power is stored up in the water of the Niagara River as it flows over Niagara Falls. By mutual agreement the governments of Canada and the United States have limited the amount of that water that can be diverted for generating electricity. But even this limited amount produces a vast amount of electricity for lighting homes and for fueling industry. Stored up in the hearts of Christian people is the unlimited power of the Holy Spirit. God "is able to do immeasurably more than all we ask or imagine, according to his power that is at work within us" (Ephesians 3:20). The spiritual potential of each believer is awesome.

Paul urges us not to quench the Spirit's fire in our lives: "Be joyful always; pray continually; give thanks in all circumstances, for this is God's will for you in Christ Jesus. Do not put out the Spirit's fire; do not treat prophecies with contempt. Test everything. Hold on to the good. Avoid every kind of evil" (1 Thessalonians 5:16-22). Notice how the things we have talked about in this book are woven into Paul's words of encouragement. Make use of the Spirit's gifts—Paul mentions joy, thankfulness, discernment. Make use of his tools, namely prayer and the Word (that is, prophecies). Make use of his power to hold to the good and avoid the evil.

Paul urges, "Be filled with the Spirit" (Ephesians 5:18). Such fullness will be ours when the Spirit remains prominent in our worship and when we give his power and guidance prominence in our lives. In this way we are bringing the Spirit the honor he is due. For as Luther writes in his explanation to the First Petition of the Lord's Prayer, we praise and glorify him "when his Word is taught in its truth and purity and we as children of God lead holy lives according to it."

Endnotes

[1]The Athanasian Creed has been used in the Western church at least since the 800s. It is included in the Lutheran Confessions of 1580 and can be found in *Christian Worship: A Lutheran Hymnal* (Milwaukee: Northwestern Publishing House, 1993), pp. 132,133.

[2]*The Glorious Koran*, Surah IV:170. Everyman's Library. (New York: Knopf, 1992), p. 115.

[3]Joseph Smith, *Doctrines of Salvation*. Quoted in Edgar Kaiser, *How to Respond to The Latter Day Saints* (St. Louis: Concordia Publishing House, 1977), p. 14.

[4]Joseph Rutherford, *Riches*. Quoted in F. E. Mayer, *The Religious Bodies of America* (St. Louis: Concordia Publishing House, 1961), p. 469.

[5]Augsburg Confession, Article I:3,4, *The Book of Concord: The Confessions of the Evangelical Lutheran Church*, translated and edited by Theodore G. Tappert (Philadelphia: Fortress Press, 1959), p. 28.

[6]Oral Roberts, *3 Most Important Steps to Your Better Health and Miracle Living* (Tulsa: Oral Roberts Evangelistic Assn., Inc., 1976), pp. 54,55.

[7]Martin Luther, as quoted in Franz Pieper, *Christian Dogmatics*, Vol. 1 (St. Louis: Concordia Pubishing House, 1950), p. 390.

[8]Martin Luther, as quoted in Pieper, *Christian Dogmatics*, Vol. 1, p. 398.

[9]Immanuel, Emmanuel, and Emanuel are alternate spellings for this name with no difference in meaning among them.

[10]In the next chapter we will see that Scripture uses the word *sanctification* also in a more limited sense to refer to the Spirit's work in leading us to live as saints. In this narrower sense *sanctification* means the Spirit leads a believer to hate sin and live a holy life filled with good works.

[11]Formula of Concord, Solid Declaration, Article V:11, Tappert, p. 560. See also Apology, Article XII:51, Tappert, p. 189.

[12]The reference is found in Siegbert Becker, *The Holy Ghost and His Work* (Milwaukee: Northwestern Publishing House, 1977), p. 19.

[13]Augsburg Confession, Article XII:4, Tappert, p. 34.

[14]John Mueller, *Christian Dogmatics* (St. Louis: Concordia Publishing House, 1955), p. 338.

[15]Formula of Concord, Solid Declaration, Article II:87, Tappert, p. 538.

[16]This error is called Pelagianism. It is named after Pelagius, a monk who lived from about A.D. 360 to about A.D. 420. He maintained that humans are born in a state of moral indifference and come to God through the strength of their own will and that grace and salvation by Christ are not necessary.

[17]This error is called semi-Pelagianism.

[18]This false teaching is called Arminianism or synergism. Jacobus Arminius lived from 1560 to 1609. He taught that humans cooperate in their conversion by free will, that is, they decide to believe. *Synergism* comes from the Greek word that means "to work with." This error teaches that people by nature are not altogether spiritually dead and that some resist God's call to faith less violently than others.

[19]Formula of Concord, Solid Declaration, Article II:89, Tappert, p. 538.

[20]Formula of Concord, Solid Declaration, Article XI:55, Tappert, p. 625.

[21]Formula of Concord, Solid Declaration, Article IV:10,11, Tappert, pp. 552,553.

[22]Formula of Concord, Solid Declaration, Article VI:20, Tappert, p. 567.

[23]Apology, Article III:42, Concordia Triglotta: The Symbolical Books of the Ev. Lutheran Church (St. Louis: Concordia Publishing House, 1921), p. 169.

[24]Martin Luther, Luther's Works, edited by Jaroslav Pelikan and Helmut T. Lehmann, American Edition, Vol. 32 (St. Louis: Concordia Publishing House; Philadelphia: Fortress Press, 1955–1986), p. 24.

[25]Apology, Article IV:365, Tappert, p. 163.

[26]Luther's Works, Vol. 33, p. 154.

[27]Mark 8:22-26 is the one exception to Jesus' instantaneous healing. Even in that case, complete healing was granted within the time span of a brief dialogue.

[28]Article VIII, as quoted in F. E. Mayer, The Religious Bodies of America (St. Louis: Concordia Pubishing House, 1961), p. 318.

[29]See pages 59, 64, and 80.

[30]William McRae, The Dynamics of Spiritual Gifts (Grand Rapids: Zondervan Publishing House, 1976), pp. 48,49.

[31]Formula of Concord, Epitome, Article III:11, Tappert, p. 474.

[32]See also Mark 3:28,29; Luke 12:10.

[33]Time, October 10, 1977, p. 76.

For Further Reading

Becker, Siegbert. *The Holy Ghost and His Work.* Milwaukee: Northwestern Publishing House, 1977.

Clement, Arthur J. *Pentecost or Pretense?* Milwaukee: Northwestern Publishing House, 1981.

Gerlach, Joel. "Glossolalia," *Wisconsin Lutheran Quarterly*, Vol. 70, No. 4 (October 1973), pp. 233-261.

Scripture Index

Romans

1 Corinthians

Subject Index